SONGDOG DIARY
66
STORIES
FROM THE ROAD

WORKS BY MICHAEL WALLIS

Oil Man
The Story of Frank Phillips and the Birth of Phillips Petroleum

Route 66
The Mother Road

Pretty Boy
The Life and Times of Charles Arthur Floyd

Way Down Yonder in the Indian Nation
Writings from America's Heartland

Mankiller
A Chief and Her People
(with Wilma Mankiller)

En Divina Luz
The Penitente Moradas of New Mexico

Beyond the Hills
The Journey of Waite Phillips

STORIES FROM THE ROAD

BY MICHAEL WALLIS & SUZANNE FITZGERALD WALLIS

Illustrated by Carol Stanton

SONG DOG BOOKS

FROM

Council Oak Publishing

Council Oak Books
Tulsa, OK 74120

First edition
00 99 98 97 96 7 6 5 4 3 2 1

Book and cover design by Carol Stanton
Illustrated by Carol Stanton

ISBN No. 1-57178-018-1

Library of Congress cataloging-in-publication data

Wallis, Michael, 1945—
Songdog diary: 66 stories from the road / by Michael Wallis & Suzanne Fitzgerald Wallis; illustrated by Carol Stanton. — 1st ed.
p. cm.
Other title: 66 stories from the road. —Sixty-six stories from the road.
ISBN 1-57178-018-1 (cloth)
1. Folklore—West (U.S.) 2. Legends— West (U.S.) 3. Popular culture—West (U.S.) 4. West (U.S.)—Social life and customs.
I. Wallis, Suzanne Fitzgerald, 1943– . II. Title.
GR109.W33 1996
398'.0978—dc20 95-43859
CIP

For the Spinners

Proud Mary

Doc

Louie

Soapy

Más

Raccoon

T.K. Flannagan

Mouse

Easy Gravy

Ed from the East

T A B L E O F

CONTENTS

AUTHORS' NOTE AND ACKNOWLEDGMENTS

The genesis of this book coincides with the creation of Songdog Books, a new Council Oak imprint. Named for the coyote — called the "songdog" by Native Americans — the imprint is a joint effort by the Wallis Group and Council Oak to produce popular nonfiction books that approach American culture with a historian's eye and a storyteller's voice. It is Songdog's mission to create in each book a narrative as alluring as a novel and as enriching as a history text, with the ultimate goal of illuminating the people and times that have created present-day American culture.

We selected the songdog as the symbol of the imprint because it is the quintessential symbol of the American West. Not only is it trickster, teacher, friend, and fool, but the coyote adapts to new circumstances with a wonderful resilience, and always sings its own song.

■

There are indeed easier missions for two people to undertake than to reach consensus on a final list of sixty-six of their favorite stories.

We began with wild abandon, generating lists of as many as 250 of what we considered major icons of the American West. We disagreed on some, but that just made for livelier debate. It was like a game of numbers, and the more icons we could remember, all the better for the West.

When it became apparent that compromises were in order, we were fortunate to enlist the assistance of several people whose expertise and opinions we value. From the fields of publishing, history, anthropology, and the arts, this cadre of "mediators" willingly entered into our debate, and they were most helpful. Our thanks go to Robert Lansdown, Lydia Lloyd Wyckoff, Sean Standingbear, Carol Haralson, Ed Wade, Jim Fitzgerald, Terrence Moore, and Clark Kimball.

Further insight was provided through the research assistance of Nancy Edwards and Dixie Haas Dooley. Their diligent search for information and concise descriptions of several dozen icons made it clear to us that our list was still far too long. The need to pare down the numbers was emphasized further when Kim Schaefer handed us her well-organized plan of action, complete with a relentless calendar of deadlines.

A phone call from Council Oak finally propelled us to look at our list in a different light. Thanks to the confidence and support of Sally Dennison, Paulette Millichap, and Michael Hightower, we were able to hone our list down to sixty-six — those familiar double sixes that represent an icon of asphalt and concrete dear to our hearts — and struggle through each other's misgivings to meet a formidable final deadline. Ultimately, out of a blend of our individual perspectives and mutual discoveries came a single voice.

We are grateful to art director Carol Stanton for carving a special design niche for our voice and giving us a timeless look. Hazel Rowena Mills has seen us through several literary efforts — once again, we appreciate her deft copy editor's pen. Kudos to Keri Beach, marketing director, for helping us make certain our song is heard. And for Judy Carr, hearty applause for managing the offices of Council Oak, and all the rest of us in the process.

When we wrestled with certain questions, we were fortunate to be able to turn to people who had the answers we needed. Thank you, Jerry and Ruth Murphey, Nick Potter, Delbert and Ruth Trew, Craig Varjabedian, Herb Haschke, and Matt Middleton.

We are particularly indebted to family and friends for their patience and encouragement. Allen Strider, Scott Fitzgerald, and Linda and Christopher Lewis were always there for us with a smile, and they understood our need to retreat like a pair of coyotes to our den. Our thanks to Nancy Hayes for her enthusiastic kinship, to

Marquita Knecht for her healthy sustenance, to Linda Adams for her eagle eye and computer expertise, and to everyone at the Wallis Group for backing this creative endeavor.

And finally, a special rub and stroke to Beatrice and Molly, our faithful feline companions, who stayed close at hand when we were at work, in spite of the canine implications of our book's title.

INTRODUCTION

Early on, we discovered that life was all the richer if it was lived in pursuit of a story. During our travels together and apart, we have met storytellers whose lore was irresistible, and we have savored every detail. As we learned our lessons in history, it was the little oddity here and there that caught our attention and brought the past to life for us. And how many times did we follow our urge to go the extra step or take the curious detour, knowing that in so doing we would be gathering fodder for stories of our own. We have been relentless in our quest, and by listening to wisdom keepers, seeking history's secrets, and turning our own lives into an adventure, we have acquired a rich collection of souvenirs, both tangible and intangible.

Our search for tantalizing tales has not been limited to the western United States, but we are tied to that part of the country. Growing up in gateway cities to the West... learning life's lessons on the brink of Mexico . . . gliding from the midlands to the Pacific shores along Route 66...simply giving in to the siren West of our imaginations all guaranteed our captivity. We invite you to share this sweet bondage.

There are entries in our diary told to us by sages we knew to trust, and by Merlin types we chose to trust. We included stories whose special quality lies not in what you will learn but in how you will remember it. And how could we resist adding an epic adventure or two about forgotten heroes? Then of course there are those tales that come out of our own experiences — when we spotted possibilities and wasted no time spinning yarns that made us into heroes in our own eyes. No matter the source, each story has become part of our song — begun in 1968 when we were in our twenties and had dreams we knew were going to come true.

This is not a diary of forbidden episodes to be kept under lock and key. It is a chronicle of maverick personalities, hidden corners, and secrets for you to relish. When you have had your fill, take inventory of your personal stash of souvenirs and set out on a hunt of your own. There are songdogs everywhere . . . you just have to listen. And along the way, don't forget to spin some stories of your own to sing.

. . . take a sad song and make it better.

— John Lennon and Paul McCartney
"Hey Jude"

A Few Good Men

Along with a few good women, what the U.S. Marine Corps is always looking for, and what the legendary Pony Express found in the reckless boys recruited to deliver the mail.

■

WANTED

Young skinny wiry fellows not over eighteen. Must be expert riders willing to risk death daily. Orphans preferred. Wages $25 per week.

— *Pony Express advertisement,* 1860

As we traverse the towering concrete and glass canyons of New York, flashes of color whiz faster than shooting stars past our taxi windows. We realize they are not comets, but young couriers bearing documents and parcels. They speed down the avenues and boulevards on bicycles and roller skates, weaving in and out of traffic with the finesse of Comanche warriors riding like the wind.

Those fleet messengers we see today put us in mind of the daring Pony Express riders delivering mail between Saint Joseph, Missouri, and Sacramento, California, for nineteen months starting on April 3, 1860. Their speedy maneuvers out on the open plains evoked even more of a response from curious stagecoach passengers straining to catch a glimpse of one of the young riders going hell-bent for leather.

Mark Twain described such a scene in *Roughing It* when he wrote:

We had a consuming desire, from the beginning, to see a pony-rider, but somehow or other all that passed us and all that met us managed to streak by us in the night, and so we heard only a whiz and a hail, and the swift phantom of the desert was gone before we could get our heads out of the windows. But now we were expecting one along every moment, and we would see him in broad daylight. Presently the driver exclaims: "Here he comes!"

Every neck is stretched further, and every eye strained wider. Away across the endless dead level of the prairie a black speck appears against the sky, and it is plain that it moves.... In a second or two it becomes a horse and rider, rising nearer — growing more and more defined — nearer and nearer, and the flutter of the hoofs comes faintly to the ear — another instant a whoop and a hurrah from our own upper deck, a wave of the rider's hand, but no reply, and man and horse burst past our excited faces, and go winging away like a belated fragment of a storm!

So sudden is it all, and so like a flash of unreal fancy, that but for the flake of white foam left quivering and perishing on a mail-sack after the vision had flashed by and disappeared, we might have doubted whether we had seen any actual horse and man at all....

Organized by Russell, Majors and Waddell, an overland freight and coach-line service, the Pony Express undoubtedly will always remain one of the more memorable episodes in the history of the American frontier. Much of that fame comes from the bold messengers who galloped across the 1,966 miles of plains, mountains, and deserts to deliver the U.S. mail.

During the brief time the Pony Express managed to stay in business, the riders endured extreme elements and other perils while carrying almost thirty-five thousand pieces of mail and earning only $100 to $150 per month, plus room and board. Remarkably, only one rider was killed and one mail sack lost.

To keep their burden light, the riders usually carried nothing more than a trusty

Colt revolver or two, and a knife. They kept their precious cargo — between forty and ninety letters — wrapped in oiled silk and crammed inside the pockets of a leather saddle cover, called a *mochila* (Spanish for "knapsack"). It was slung over the saddle and easily removed when the riders changed mounts at relay stations every fifteen miles along their path.

The company issued each young man a leather-bound bible and required him to sign an oath which read:

I hereby swear, before the great and living God, that during my engagement, and while I am an employee of Russell, Majors & Waddell, I will, under no circumstances, use profane language; that I will drink no intoxicating liquors; that I will not quarrel or fight with any other employee of this firm; and that in every respect, I will conduct myself honestly, faithful to my duties, and so direct my acts as to win the confidence of my employers. So help me God.

But even the Almighty could not keep the Pony Express alive. Although the method of mail delivery was fast and efficient, the price of operation was too costly. After losing more than $200,000, Russell, Majors and Waddell decided to discontinue the service. Most of the riders were not surprised. For a long time, they had been delivering progress reports to work crews erecting transcontinental telegraph poles. On October 26, 1861, just two days after the nation was linked by the "singing wires," the Pony Express officially ceased operations.

The trails worn across prairie and mountain have faded, and the old stables in Saint Joseph house the Pony Express Museum, where memories are stored. Still, the spirit of those nimble "pony boys" gallops to life every time our faithful postman tiptoes up the icy sidewalk or an express delivery truck screeches to a halt in front of our house — or, from the corner of our eyes, we catch the blur of a courier hurtling down the streets of New York "like a belated fragment of a storm."

Ansel Adams

1902–1984. Photographer.

▪

If Ansel Adams, a maestro of light and shadow with his camera, had taken only one photograph — "Moonrise, Hernandez, New Mexico" — we would still consider him one of our icons.

Certainly the best-known photograph of the many images he captured of the American West, the compelling "Moonrise" was taken on October 31, 1941, while Adams, his son Michael, and photographer Cedric Wright motored from Colorado to Carlsbad, New Mexico. The party was on U.S. 84 in the Chama River Valley about six miles north of Española, New Mexico, when Adams glanced to the left near the village of Hernandez and caught a glimpse of the rising autumn moon. As the moonlight played on the village graveyard, Adams slammed on the brakes and rushed to set up his eight-by-ten camera.

"The situation was desperate," Adams later wrote, "the low sun was trailing the edge of the clouds in the west, and shadow would soon dim the white crosses."

There was time to take only a single photograph. But that was enough.

Alcatraz

A twelve-acre island in San Francisco Bay, California, named Isla de los Alcatraces (Island of the Pelicans) in 1769 by the Spanish for the big white birds that congregated there. Former site of a maximum-security federal penitentiary.

▪

If you're going to San Francisco, be sure to take a long look at the Golden Gate Bridge, but also check out the place that's commonly called "the Rock." You can see it from Fisherman's Wharf. Better yet, take a boat tour and travel a little more than a mile across the choppy bay waters for an even closer inspection.

Sometimes in the dying sunlight when the fog moves in, Alcatraz seems to be only a mirage. It is not. Once a sanctuary for gulls and pelicans, this irregular oblong hump of barren sandstone, stuck in the waters between San Francisco and Sausalito, became an inhumane warehouse for the living dead — an island of hate.

In the 1800s, the U.S. government turned Alcatraz into a military prison for Confederate captives, convict soldiers, and Native Americans who were considered renegades. To this day, Apaches in Arizona keep alive a woeful dirge that tells the story of one of their warriors who dared go against the white man and was dragged off in manacles to the lonely island.

After the 1906 San Francisco earthquake, the city's jail population was taken to Alcatraz for safekeeping. By World War I, conscientious objectors resided in the island's honeycomb of cellblocks. In 1933, Alcatraz was transformed into a high-security penitentiary for the nation's most incorrigible convicts. There was no rehabilitation; it was a holding place for the damned. During twenty-nine years, 1,545 inmates were sentenced to five-by-nine-foot cells in the prison known as the End of the Line, the Dumping Ground, America's Devil's Island, the Garbage Can, and Hellcatraz. Celebrity prisoners included Al "Scarface" Capone, Alvin "Creepy" Karpis, George "Machine Gun" Kelly, and Robert "Birdman of Alcatraz" Stroud. In 1963, the site was closed as a prison.

In 1969, Alcatraz was reclaimed once again as a sanctuary. A group of Native American activists occupied the island for nineteen months, claiming it as Indian land. Alcatraz became a symbol to attract attention to the federal government's long history of mistreatment of Indian people. The Rock had come full circle — from sanctuary to prison to sanctuary.

Today, visitors see the somber cell house, barren sandstone, and traces of Indian graffiti. They hear foghorns, the protesting gulls, and the soft cries of thousands of songdog ghosts.

Although Alcatraz would ultimately not remain a sovereign Indian nation, the incredible publicity generated by the occupation served all of us well by dramatizing the injustices that the modern Native Americans have endured at the hands of white America. The Alcatraz experience nurtured a sense among us that anything was possible — even, perhaps, justice for native people.

— Wilma Mankiller and Michael Wallis
Mankiller: A Chief and Her People

Aspen

A fast-growing but short-lived tree found on mountainsides and mesas throughout the West, especially in areas previously scorched by fire. The trees are known best for their annual show of color in autumn, when their fluttering leaves turn golden yellow, or sometimes orange and crimson. Also, a town in Colorado founded in 1879 as Ute City and renamed Aspen the following year. This former west-central Colorado mining settlement has become a center for winter sports and summer cultural activities.

▪

Planning is everything when it comes to that narrow window of time in the autumn when the shimmering aspen leaves are at their peak.

One year, in our exuberance to capture that special chrome-yellow moment of seasonal ritual, we departed Santa Fe in the predawn hours for the nearby mountain meadows splotched with groves of aspen. We followed an old logging road off the main mountain path only to discover that it was still too dark to see the aspens in all their glory. To make matters worse, we found ourselves on a stretch of treacherous ice. Our car slid precariously close to the edge of the road, but stopped on the brink of disaster. We hardly dared to breathe for what seemed like an eternity, for fear any movement would cause the car to tumble over the mountainside. At long last, dawn's early light appeared, and just for an instant the sun's rays struck the aspen in a way we had not seen before or since. Then the sun grew stronger, and before long the ice that bound us melted, and we continued on our way.

The trees that rise like phoenix birds from the ashes and paint the slopes golden each autumn also have lent their name to a settlement where men once sought not gold, but silver. This town can be found high in the Rocky Mountains, about two hundred miles from Denver.

Set among the steep slopes in the valley of the Roaring Fork River is Aspen, one of the nation's premier ski resorts. Unlike Vail, Crested Butte, and many of the other skiing meccas, this playground for the rich and famous has a history steeped in culture.

From its earliest days as a mining camp, Aspen has been famous. In the 1880s, the town prospered from the reef of silver hidden beneath the land. By 1882, when the population had swelled to almost twelve thousand, the Smuggler Mine had made Aspen the world's largest silver camp, a center of the arts and commerce, and the third-largest city in Colorado. During those boom years, Aspen boasted a dozen churches, six newspapers, two breweries, a theater, an opera house, streetcars, and the three-story Hotel Jerome, considered by some people to be the handsomest hotel on the Western Slope and "the best west of Kansas City."

The bottom fell out in 1893. As suddenly as a January blizzard, disaster struck when the silver market collapsed. Within a matter of weeks, almost every silver mine in Colorado had closed.

After a half century of struggle, Aspen's second coming arrived immediately after World War II when industrialist Walter Paepcke and his wife, Elizabeth, moved to the mountain hamlet. The Paepckes became a driving force behind the Aspen revival through their restoration of Victorian architecture and their infusion of culture, which led to the founding of the Aspen Music Festival and the Aspen Institute for Humanistic Studies. Symphony orchestras came to play, and such notables as Albert Schweitzer and Thornton Wilder made appearances. At the same time, Aspen was developing international attention as a chic ski resort.

Swarms of movie stars and "beautiful people" now clog the streets once walked by miners and silver kings. It is our hope that they remember to observe that brief span of time that comes around each year, when the trees that gave their town its name turn to gold.

Astrodome

Opened in Houston, Texas, in 1965 and officially named Harris County Domed Stadium, the Astrodome was the world's first indoor stadium.

■

We are not sure if we should curse or bless the Astrodome — that giant air-conditioned arena that gave the world AstroTurf in place of God's own green grass.

On April 9, 1965, President Lyndon B. Johnson was on hand to watch an exhibition duel between the New York Yankees and Houston Astros — the first baseball game ever played indoors.

Erected on what had once been perfectly good grazing land for cattle, the Astrodome seats as many as sixty-six thousand people, with parking for thirty thousand vehicles. Besides sports events, entertainment extravaganzas, and conventions, the Astrodome — which could hold an eighteen-story building inside — is the site of the Houston Stock Show and Rodeo.

This architectural landmark has become part of a $100 million entertainment complex which, along with Astrohall and Astroarena, is known as Astrodomain. We have stalked the dimensions of the place. One time when delivering some friends to a convention, we even boldly drove our car right inside, screeching to a halt in the middle of the arena floor. Looking all around us from that vantage point, it was easy to see that the 'Dome is Texas Big ... Astronomically Big.

Atomic Bomb

A nuclear weapon capable of great destruction which produces a powerful explosion through the rapid release of large amounts of energy as a result of reactions involving atomic nuclei.

■

In 1970, we climbed the steep mesas at Hopi. On the trail ahead of us, we caught glimpses of some Hopi girls and heard their soft laughter. By the time we reached the Third Mesa village of Hotevilla ("The Place of a Spring Inside a Cave Where a Low Entrance Might Scratch Your Back"), the girls had vanished, and all we heard were the whispers of prayer eagles tethered to adobe roofs.

Then new sounds came to us on the wind. We heard spoken language, and soon we saw a cluster of Hopi leaders and a group of Japanese men and women in their finest suits and dresses. The visitors had survived the horrors of the atomic-bomb destruction at Hiroshima in 1945. Their leader was a retired university president who had lost his family and most of his students in the horrible blast. Like the others with him, the old man's skin was discolored, and he bore the permanent scars of war.

The Japanese were on a mission of peace, a delegation seeking communities of people who also sought and valued a peaceful way of life. Naturally, their journey had brought them to these villages in northeastern Arizona, home of the Hopi, whose very name means "peaceful ones."

Almost three decades earlier, the atomic bomb had emerged hundreds of miles east of Hopi. It was perfected in our beloved New Mexico, on a series of mesas created by flowing volcanic lava — in a place born out of hell called Los Alamos. Ironically, this secret enclave of scientists and research laboratories evolved out of World War II in the "Land of Enchantment," a magnet for artists, writers, and creative forces. Surrounded by a barbed-wire fence twelve feet high, this isolated hamlet in the Jemez Mountains forty-five miles northwest of Santa Fe became home during the early 1940s for the Manhattan Project scientists charged with the development of the atomic bomb.

On July 16, 1945, at 5:29:45 A.M., the first atomic device test — dubbed Project Trinity — took place at White Sands Proving Ground, northwest of Alamogordo in southeastern New Mexico. When detonated, the explosion vaporized the hundred-foot-tall steel tower on which the bomb was hung. Desert sands were fused by the blast into a green rock called "trinitite." The rush of air ten miles away knocked men from their feet, and the blinding nuclear flash was seen as far away as El Paso and Santa Fe. Windows were shattered in Silver City, 120 miles from ground zero.

The rehearsal was a success. Just weeks later, on the morning of August 6, 1945, the United States unleased this terrible fury when the American B-29 *Enola Gay* dropped an atomic bomb on the Japanese city of Hiroshima. Three days later, another B-29, *Bock's Car*, released an atomic bomb over Nagasaki. More than 100,000 persons were killed outright, hundreds of thousands more were left maimed and homeless — and the war was effectively ended.

Sometimes we pause in one of the Hispanic villages along the High Road to Taos in the Sangre de Cristo Mountains. We peer across time and space at the distant twinkling lights of Los Alamos, cradle of the A-bomb and that terrible radioactive mushroom cloud which for some people has become the ultimate symbol of the twentieth century. Neither that hideous cloud nor childhood memories from the 1950s of backyard bomb shelters, Geiger counters, and "duck-and-cover" drills in school classrooms comes to mind.

We choose to turn our thoughts elsewhere. We think of the wooded canyons below the Atomic City, where cliff dwellings and ceremonial kivas from long ago remain. We think of the lofty cottonwoods along the acequias and banks of the Rio Grande. We are struck that Los Alamos and Alamogordo — the two New Mexico sites so closely associated with nuclear weapons — bear the Spanish names for cottonwood, the symbol of life in the arid Southwest.

But mostly, one image from our own past remains indelible in our minds.

We recall those Hopi elders and their Japanese visitors, who shared only the universal language of peace. We will forever see them gathered below those majestic eagles that preened in the sun on that high desert mesa. For that we are thankful.

The bomb that fell on Hiroshima fell on
America too.
It fell on no city, no munition plants,
no docks.
It erased no church, vaporized no
public buildings,
reduced no man to his atomic elements.
But it fell, it fell
It burst. It shook the land.

God have mercy on our children.
God have mercy on America.

—Hermann Hagedorn
"The Bomb That Fell on America"

Beverly Hills

A residential community of southern California at the foot of the Santa Monica Mountains, founded in 1907 and incorporated as a city in 1914.

▪

We remember Beverly Hills from our westward journeys down Route 66. The venerable Mother Road uses the alias Santa Monica Boulevard in this ritzy neck of the woods as it nears its terminus at the Pacific shore. When we motor past the posh palaces and smart shops of Beverly Hills, we are reminded that this mecca for the rich and famous was carved out of an old Spanish land grant covered with sagebrush.

Less than six square miles in area, Beverly Hills was the brainchild of entrepreneur Burton E. Green, a land developer who, in the early 1900s, named his newly created California city for his hometown of Beverly Farms, Massachusetts. The fledgling motion-picture industry was booming in nearby Hollywood. When Douglas Fairbanks and Mary Pickford came to Beverly Hills and built their Pickfair estate in 1919, other celluloid luminaries soon followed, including Tom Mix, Will Rogers, John Barrymore, Gloria Swanson, and Rudolph Valentino.

Always a city of superlatives, Beverly Hills developed into an oasis completely surrounded by the megalopolis of Los Angeles. It was known as the most prestigious address in America. City promoters touted the community as a trendsetter in fashion, lifestyle, and beauty. But we like what Ray Riegert had to say in his book, *Hidden Southern California: The Adventurer's Guide:*

It's a rags-to-riches town with a lot of Horatio Alger stories to tell. The world capitol of wealth and glamour, Beverly Hills is a place in which driving a BMW makes you a second-class citizen and where the million-dollar houses are in the poorer part of town. The community with more gardeners per capita than any other United States city, Beverly Hills is one of the few spots outside Texas where flaunting your money is still considered good taste. A facelift here is as common as a haircut and many of the residents look like they've been embalmed for the past thirty years.

Beverly Hills will always play host to royalty and swarms of tourists all seeking the ultimate experience — whether it's at the Polo Lounge in the famed Beverly Hills Hotel (built in 1912 at Sunset Boulevard and Beverly Drive), in one of the trendy restaurants, or at the splashy designer boutiques with outrageous prices along the three blocks of Rodeo Drive (pronounced roh-DAY-oh) in the heart of this city that is simply *too much.*

Billy the Kid

1859-1881. Cowboy, gambler, cattle thief , and legendary outlaw, born in New York City. Known as William Bonney, Henry McCarty, Henry Antrim, and "the Kid."

▪

It was Christmas Eve, 1969, and we were deep in the heart of New Mexico's "Billy the Kid" country. When our car broke down, we hitched a ride to Socorro and waited outside a garage while a diligent mechanic attempted to set things straight. As we shared a cup of whiskey-laced thermos coffee, we spied a figure in the night shadows. It was an old man, bowlegged and scarred, with gun-metal gray hair that hung to his shoulders. He commenced talking to us just as though we were old pals he saw every day. He spoke of dust storms and blizzards and acts of God, but mostly he stuck to the times he knew best — those wild old days when he was young and on the prowl.

The old man spoke of range wars and shootings and jail breaks. He talked of Billy the Kid, and said it was hard to separate legend from truth when it came to the young man who had died at the tender age of twenty-one. "I knew the Kid," the old man told us straight out. "I knew the Kid as well as my own brother."

Eighty-eight years had passed since Billy had died at the hands of Sheriff Pat Garrett. But we chose not to doubt the claim of the old-timer whose piercing eyes held a glint of truth. Maybe it was the circumstances — the night before Christmas, under a big white moon, with just enough Jack Daniel's to tease our imagination.

Nine years later in Austin, we met Jarvis Garrett, son of the legendary lawman. He was only three years old in 1908 when his father was ambushed and shot dead while he was urinating alongside a road near Las Cruces, New Mexico. Jarvis — thin and wiry — told us he had a faint memory of his father's wake. He told us most of the books and movies about his father and Billy the Kid were worthless. "There are so many legends, so many falsehoods," he said. "Writers let their imaginations work overtime." Then he allowed us to hold the .44-caliber Colt revolver his father had used to write history.

After we said so long to Garrett, we talked about our brush with history. We also thought back to that mysterious old man in Socorro who had flitted through our lives like a catnap dream with his stories of America's quintessential outlaw.

Black Gold

A term of endearment for crude oil used by those in the oil business in Oklahoma, Texas, and elsewhere.

■

pe•tro•le•um. *a rock; an oily, liquid solution of hydrocarbons, yellowish-green to black in color, occurring naturally in the rock strata of certain geological formations: when fractionally distilled it yields paraffin, kerosene, benzene, naphtha, fuel oil, gasoline, etc.*

— *Webster's New World Dictionary*

For many years, Plains Indians noticed the black ooze percolating from the earth. They scooped it from springs or used feathers to skim it from tiny pools formed by buffalo hooves in the mud. The Indians considered oil a good cure for rheumatism, and they rubbed it into wounds on their hunting ponies. In Indian Territory, some enterprising Cherokees peddled oil as a natural elixir, but besides employing its curative powers and using oil-soaked cattails for torches, the Indians had no other real purpose for the stuff.

That all changed with the coming of the white men. Just like the forty-niners who searched for real gold, wildcatters moved into present Oklahoma, Texas, and throughout the West by the early twentieth century. They prospected for new deposits of wealth in the form of rich crude oil that came to be known as "black gold."

Some of the biggest oil finds were in Oklahoma's Burbank Field, in the rolling grasslands that had become the home of the Osage tribe.

Osage soothsayers and men of magic knew the land was special and the hills were filled with mystery. They also believed that below the coal-black soil, locked in the deep recesses of the earth, was a treasure that could help the tribe if they held on to their land. One visionary said he saw, clear as a summer sky, the death of the old ways. He saw visions of more white men coming and he could even picture their strange machines, snorting and bellowing as if they were iron buffaloes. He said the white men would come like a wave of water. "You cannot stop that wave," he told the old Osage chiefs. They nodded and sat silent beneath the night sky.

— Michael Wallis
Oil Man: The Story of Frank Phillips and the Birth of Phillips Petroleum

Broken Wheel Colony

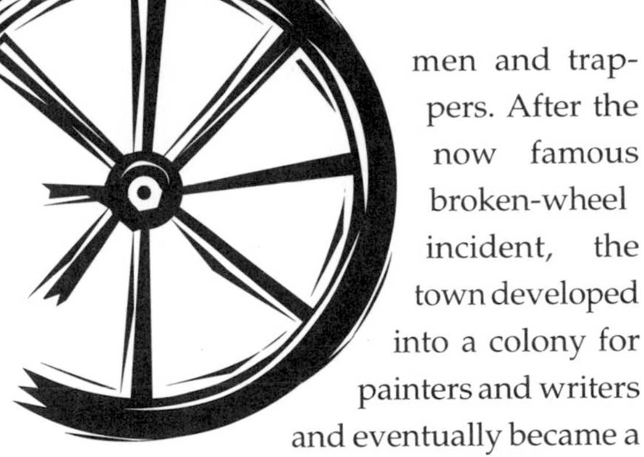

Symbol for the famed Taos Art Colony, the name came about in 1898 when painters Ernest Blumenschein and Bert Phillips, fueled by glowing reports from fellow artist Joseph Henry Sharp, journeyed through New Mexico. Thirty miles north of the Taos valley, a wheel on their wagon broke. On the flip of a coin, Blumenschein was picked to ride horseback with the broken wheel to the closest town for repairs. The name of that town was Taos. Enchanted with the quaint village and struck by the beauty of the area, Blumenschein and Phillips decided to remain in Taos. Later, Sharp joined them, followed by several other notable artists who eventually helped organize the Taos Society of Artists.

Formally known as Don Fernando de Taos, the community had been settled by Spanish colonists early in the seventeenth century. It became a trade center for the Spanish and for Pueblo and Comanche Indians, and by the nineteenth century was known as a headquarters for mountain men and trappers. After the now famous broken-wheel incident, the town developed into a colony for painters and writers and eventually became a popular tourist destination and ski resort.

Taos Pueblo, or San Geronimo de Taos, is a few miles northeast of the town plaza. Hundreds of traditional people still live in large adobe dwellings that are popular images for postcards.

▪

On the very first day of 1970, we climbed into a battered red Chevy pickup truck in Santa Fe and struck out for Taos. Joining us was our brother Jimmy, between boot camp and Vietnam, along with a band of creative coconspirators — Proud Mary, Louie, Easy Gravy, Soapy, Ed from the East, and the pickup's owner, Matt, who during the years of the Vietnam draft lived under the alias of T.K. Flannagan. Filled with much of the spirit that drove Ken Kesey and his Merry Pranksters, we dubbed ourselves the Spinners.

As gypsy-footed as our name and as spontaneous as our freshly drafted New Year's resolutions, we decided in a heartbeat to leave. Some of us wore remnants of our old army and marine uniforms, others were clad in vintage cloaks and plumed hats and an assortment of colorful caps, mittens, and costumes. Among us, we had a few dollars, a couple of old blankets, a bit of rum, and a lot of hope. A tarot card — the Fool — dangled from the rearview mirror.

It was bitterly cold, and snow covered the ground. In deference to the temperature, which hovered in the teens, we didn't take the preferred High Road to Taos through a string of mountain villages. Instead, we chose the more direct route, on the highway that slices through canyons and rock walls flanking the icy Rio Grande.

We were on a quest, hoping to find a woman we had heard and read about. We believed she could help us understand all we would need to know to start a renaissance. We were young and filled with optimism. No challenge seemed too great — not a seventy-five-mile ride on a frigid winter's day in the back of a pickup, not the ordeal of securing shelter for the night, not even the rather lofty notion that the Spinners could launch a major cultural movement.

▪

Taos has always been a mecca for those in need of sustenance — be it potent whiskey to warm the hearts and souls of mountain men of long ago, or enchilada platters and baskets of sopaipillas for the herds of tourists and skiers of the present.

The northern New Mexican hamlet also has been a suitable location to inspire and stir imaginations. At one time or another, all sorts of folks and every conceivable type of artist — painters, sculptors, poets, playwrights, actors, composers — have journeyed to Taos to see if the brilliant sky, mysterious dark mountains, and surrounding mesas studded with fragrant sagebrush would cause their creative sap to rise and flow.

We knew that wisdom keepers abided there, not only at the ancient pueblo but also scattered throughout the adobe town. In time, we would come to know many of them, including survivors of Taos art patroness Mabel Dodge Luhan's inner circle. Some of them became our friends. But on this first day of a new and fresh decade, we raced on in the dying sunlight looking for only one — an elderly, deaf English painter named Dorothy Brett.

Although she had lived as an artist in Taos since the 1920s, the woman we sought began her life during a time that seemed light-years before, in the stately court of Queen Victoria.

▪

Born in 1883 into a privileged family of wealth and position in the pomp and circumstance of Victorian aristocracy, Dorothy Eugenie Brett was the first daughter of Reginald Baliol Brett, Viscount Esher, a trusted member of Parliament and adviser to the storied old monarch. Raised in the elegance and leisure of Queen Victoria's court, the young Brett — thanks to her mother, the former Eleanor Van-de-Meyer — was tutored in the classical tradition. Her schooling included dancing lessons in Windsor Castle, but she proved to be somewhat awkward and once knocked over the stool where the diminutive queen had placed her feet.

In 1902, Brett's father organized the coronation of King Edward VII, and the following year Brett made her debut at court. One of her first escorts was young Winston Churchill. It did not go well. Brett found Churchill rude and offensive. In addition, she was beginning to lose her hearing, and the large brass ear trumpet she later named Toby made Brett the object of scorn and ridicule on the part of her snooty father as well as upper-class British society. None of the trappings of court life appealed to the fiery young woman who had no intention of ending up Lady Brett but who early on decided to follow her creative feelings and become a painter.

Much to her family's dismay, Brett left court and never returned. She followed her heart and enrolled at London's Slade School of Art, where she trained for four years, developing an unconventional style that combined the visionary world with a manner largely her own. She also established a new set of friends — including Middleton Murray, Katherine Mansfield, Aldous Huxley, Bertrand Russell, and Virginia Woolf — who were much more to her liking than the stuffy types she had had to endure in royal circles.

In 1924, Brett came to the United States with English novelist D.H. Lawrence and his wife, Freida. They were drawn to Taos, which Lawrence described as "one of the magnetic centers of the earth."

Brett had been introduced to Lawrence in London in 1915. They immediately became close friends, or as Brett later told us, "Something sparked between us." Lawrence eased Brett's painful shyness and caused her to feel that time spent with him was "almost unbearably exciting."

Lawrence was beginning to attract attention in literary circles, but he suffered from tuberculosis and sought relief through quixotic wanderings around the globe. His traveling had kept Lawrence and his friend Brett apart until 1923, when he and Freida returned to Great Britain from the United States.

The Lawrences' last U.S. address had been Taos — the art community tucked away in the Sangre de Cristo Mountains. Taos was the cultural domain of Mabel Dodge Luhan, a spunky patroness of the arts who lured intellectually attractive artists to her adopted home of New Mexico. Lawrence had been one of those whom Mabel had snared. Although much tension had developed between the Lawrences and their hostess, the temperamental novelist believed New Mexico could be fertile ground for his so-called Rananim — an ideal community or utopian colony of artists. Lawrence described his colony as one "based, not on poverty but on riches, not on humility but on pride, not on sacrifice but upon complete fulfillment in the flesh of all strong desire, not in heaven but on earth."

In 1924, at a now famous "last supper" in a London cafe, Lawrence plied a gathering of his associates with enough of his fiery charisma and strong drink to convince them of a Rananim's importance. By the end of that evening, everyone present vowed to make the trip to Taos with Lawrence. Later that year, when the ship finally sailed to the United States, Lawrence and Freida had but a single colonist accompanying them — Brett.

▪

It was this journey, one that lasted a lifetime for Brett, that drew us to her in 1970. We wanted to know whether she had found that Rananim and how, with the Lawrences, she had fueled that creative spirit.

After spending a less than idyllic night wrapped in blankets and sleeping bags on the earthen floor of a hippie commune, the Spinners ventured into the brilliant morning sunlight. We found Brett at her home in El Prado, four miles north of the Taos plaza. Her cluttered studio was filled with easels, canvases, and books. She invited all of us into a large circular room, and we sat around her and began a conversation that would continue off and on for more than seven years.

Brett told us of her coming to Taos with the Lawrences, and of those turbulent times with Mabel Dodge Luhan and the creative geniuses who flocked to the mountain hamlet. She gave us her suggestions about how to launch a renaissance, and shared her opinions about the pros and cons of a Rananim.

She told us that the utopia Lawrence wished to create never became a reality, but that did not halt the creative process. "People should live apart and do their work — their writing, painting, composing — and then gather at certain times to share and discuss their ideas, and nourish one another," Brett said. "Where this gathering takes place doesn't really matter."

We took Brett's words to heart. The bond we had formed as a group — Spinners in search of a creative beginning — was strengthened by the revelation that we had to pursue our dreams as individuals. A few of us returned time and again to visit with Brett and absorb her wisdom and inspiration.

Brett died in 1977. She was ninety-three years old and had outlived her beloved Lawrence by more than forty-seven years; she had outlived most of her friends and critics by decades. Her home and studio where we had gathered on so many occasions became Brett House, a restaurant for tourists to dine on sautéed chicken breasts and crème brûlée with fresh raspberries.

Through the years, the Spinners have moved in different directions. We are scattered across the land. We reside in New York, San Francisco, and small towns and cities throughout the West. We are writers, poets, painters, photographers, editors, and teachers. All of us are still dreamers.

Every once in a while we gather, often in a big city or in New Mexico, where it all began. Sometimes we find ourselves together in Oklahoma at our home where, among the creative litter, are photographs of that first day of 1970 and portraits of Brett and the other old magicians who taught us so much.

I think New Mexico was the greatest experience from the outside world that I have ever had. It certainly changed me forever....The moment I saw the brilliant proud morning shine high up over the deserts of Santa Fe, something stood still in my soul, and I started to attend..... In the magnificent fierce morning of New Mexico one sprang awake, a new part of the soul woke up suddenly, and the old world gave way to the new.

— D.H. Lawrence
Survey Graphic, 1931

Buffalo

North America's largest native animal, once found in astronomical numbers, especially on the Great Plains, actually not a buffalo at all, but a bison. The name *buffalo* originated with early Spaniards, who mistakenly called the huge beast *búfalo* after the wild oxen of India and Africa.

▪

One autumn morning in 1993, we were among those blessed to witness the return of the buffalo to Oklahoma's Osage Hills. The first call of songbirds on the wind rippling across bluestem and Indian grasses was interrupted as three hundred buffalo lumbered out of the fog to reclaim their place in the scheme of life. The herd passed in review and disappeared into the largest stretch of tallgrass prairie remaining on the continent.

The "monarchs of the plains" once dominated tribal life among Native American people, but were virtually exterminated by white trophy hunters and "buffalo runners," hired to supply railroad crews with fresh meat. "Buffalo were dark rich clouds moving upon the rolling hills and plains of America," writes Acoma Pueblo poet Simon Ortiz. "And then the flashing steel came upon bone and flesh."

By 1889, the buffalo, once estimated at sixty million, totaled fewer than six hundred. The slaughter finally ended and the buffalo was saved, thanks to the efforts of the American Bison Society, formed in 1905, and other wildlife conservationists.

The buffalo has thundered back softly from near extinction. Today, more than thirty thousand thrive in public and private herds. That's why we uttered our own prayer of thanks on that autumn morning in the Osage at the Nature Conservancy's Tallgrass Prairie Preserve, when the buffalo came home. We will always see the last two of that herd — a watchful calf running alongside a shaggy old bull, with massive hump and head carried low. The past and the present were before us.

Bugaboos

Something that causes needless fear or anxiety, this unusual term was used frequently by loggers and prospectors to describe the forbidding granite towers dotting the glacial gorges and snow-domed peaks of a rugged range of Canadian Rockies. "It gives me the bugaboos," is how they usually put it. Hence the name is used for a glacier and for that particular range of the Purcell Mountains in western Canada.

▪

True love is like ghosts, which everybody talks about and few have seen.

— François, Duc de La Rochefoucauld
Reflections; or, Sentences and Moral Maxims

We will never forget the morning we met Sam. It was in August and we were in the mountain country of western Canada, exploring the far reaches of the Bugaboos, heli-hiking to the peaks of the Cariboos, and traversing blue-green glaciers and timeless ice fields.

We came upon Sam at the Banff Springs Hotel — that fine old castle with thick stone walls, surrounded by fir and pine, which rises eleven stories above the confluence of the Bow and Spray Rivers.

Way back in 1887, the Canadian Pacific Railway decided to build the hotel in Banff, the famous resort town of southwestern Alberta, a prairie province not far from the British Columbia border in the heart of the Canadian Rockies. Additions to the hotel were made almost every year. Starting in about 1910 and continuing throughout the 1920s, much of the original structure was demolished and rebuilt.

It is still one of Canada's finest old railroad hotels. Most travelers come to the Banff Springs in sedans or campers. A few arrive in airplanes and glide in on grass runways built for Benny Goodman when the famed bandleader and his orchestra came to serenade the hotel's guests.

There is room for at least seventeen hundred guests at the Banff Springs, where all the bellmen wear kilts, a bagpiper salutes the sunset each evening, and ladies and gentlemen don tweeds and woolens after high tea to play croquet on the immaculate front lawn. Those not interested in skiing, hiking, or horseback riding may go to one of the swimming pools or tennis courts. Inside the huge hotel are busy kitchens and dining rooms, comfortable bars and lounges, and scores of gift shops. And on the eighth floor is Sam.

We heard stories about Sam McCauley, the ghostly bellman, even before our luggage reached our room. Of all the ghosts who dwell at the Banff Springs Hotel — and we were led to believe there may be several — Sam is the most acclaimed and the most visible.

A desk clerk told us that Sam had worked as a bellman there for decades, and was well remembered as a cantankerous fellow who always vowed he would never leave the drafty old hotel. Sam kept his word. Although he had died more than a decade before our visit, it appeared that he was still about. The desk clerk swore to us that Sam was still there. So did the bellman toting our bags, and so did the bell captain, who knew Sam quite well in life and apparently afterward. "He's much friendlier now," the bell captain assured us.

Fascinated with the ghost stories, we sought out more staff members after dinner and asked them to tell us what they knew about Sam. We learned about all sorts of unexplained happenings at the hotel — bright lights suddenly appearing in rooms, people responding to the sound of keys in their doors only to find no one there, and bartenders in the Rob Roy Room hearing a man singing in the washroom long after closing. We also were told that there were constant reports of an elderly bellman fitting Sam's description who appeared out of nowhere to help someone. Sometimes it was late at night, after room service had shut down, and Sam suddenly showed up with a lifesaving midnight snack for a ravenous guest.

On other occasions, Sam went to the rescue of stranded guests who had reached their rooms but forgotten their keys. Often, visitors would leave envelopes of money for Sam at the front desk. "Just give this to the nice older bellman who was so helpful," they told the smiling clerk. Everyone who knew Sam in life agreed with the bell captain that the old bellhop was much friendlier as he made his ghostly rounds — principally, and for no earthly reason that anyone could give us — on the eighth floor. That was where we would most likely encounter Sam, they told us.

Our minds remained open and our ears cocked, but no shining lights or keys in the door interrupted our sleep. If Sam was not interested in visiting us, then we would locate him. We rose before daybreak and left our room on the third floor to find Sam. The hotel was silent and our imaginations were strained as we approached the elevators. Suddenly, before we could even touch the buttons, the elevator door opened with a startling ring. To our shock and amazement, the only floor light glowing on the selection panel was for floor number eight — Sam's domain. We looked at each other and rose to the occasion. We stepped inside, and the elevator shot straight up to the eighth floor, came to a halt, and the doors opened.

It was much warmer on the eighth floor. That was the first thing we noticed as we crept down the halls. At the end of one corridor, we were attracted to a window where the first hints of dawn could be seen. We opened the window and climbed out onto the fire escape. It was cool and shadowy, and we held each other and watched the low white clouds hugging the river and valley before us. We heard the poetry of the water as it tore through rock and time. It was a special moment — perhaps, we later thought, the best single moment we had had that entire year. Then, in an instant, the sun grew stronger and the scene shifted and changed.

We climbed back inside and walked down the hall, hand in hand, to the elevators. This time, the only button light aglow was the third floor. We smiled and returned to our room. Later that day, when we checked out of the hotel, we silently thanked Sam for that moment of beauty on a chilly August morning high above the Bow River at the Banff Springs Hotel.

We trusted that the contents of the envelope we left behind would be put to good use on some future evening, when from out of the shadows an old man in a double-breasted plaid jacket, with white hair and a gleam in his eye, would buy a round of drinks for a table of guests in the Rob Roy Room. We could almost hear him singing.

Cain's Ballroom

Located at 423 North Main Street in Tulsa, Oklahoma, the world-famous Cain's Ballroom is acknowledged as the birthplace of an American music phenomenon known as western swing.

■

Every city we have called home in the American West has at least one edifice that defines that particular place for us. It may not be the most pristine example of architecture, or is it necessarily the biggest or the best. But it serves as a symbol for us and helps to shape that town's identity.

In Austin, it is the big, pink granite capitol building. And in Santa Fe, it is a toss-up between our beloved La Fonda, a former Harvey House at the end of the Santa Fe Trail, and the Woolworth store, a bastion of honesty on the plaza that survives despite the surrounding phalanx of chic galleries and fancy shops. Saint Louis, where so many historic buildings survive from various layers of the city's history, is dominated by the stunning Gateway Arch, but our choice is nearby Monks Mound, across the Mississippi, not far from Cahokia, Illinois. The ancient mound is still the best vantage point for those who want to get the right perspective of the river city. In El Paso, an old buff brick residence on Rim Road in the heights above downtown — although gone from the family — will always be our center of gravity in the border city.

One of our signature landmarks in Tulsa has to be Cain's Ballroom.

We did not truly appreciate Cain's until we moved to Tulsa, the cultural capital of Oklahoma and a city replete with stunning architecture including scores of art deco gems — stately mansions, corporate palaces, and cathedrals. Cain's cannot claim an elaborate architectural design, but what transpired inside the building that has been described as "a blue-collar palace" built of limestone transformed a rather ordinary structure into an icon for the world of music. As one writer once put it, "Cain's is Western Swing's own Alamo."

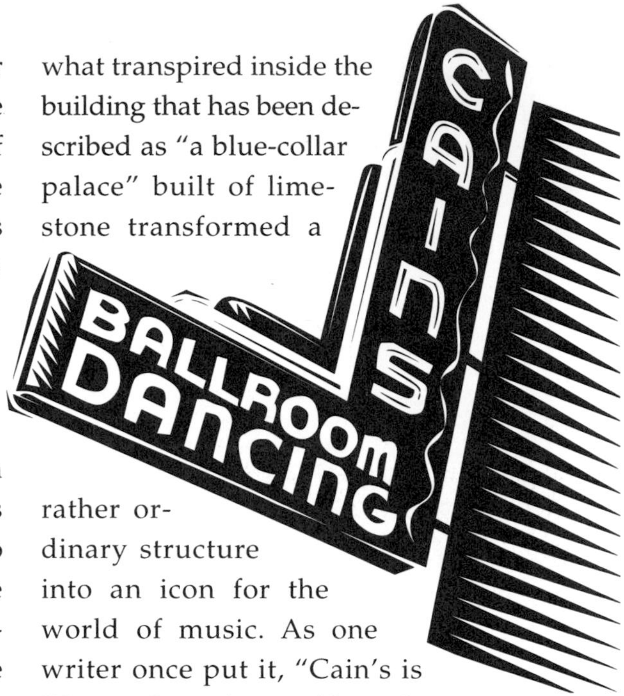

It was originally built to house an automobile dealership, but before the business could open, a change of plans transformed it into a dance hall dubbed the Louvre. Later it became known as Cain's Dancing Academy, where Madison "Daddy" Cain taught Tulsans how to waltz and do the Charleston.

By the middle of the Great Depression, the big wooden dance floor mounted on truck springs was crowded with cowboys and cowgirls and honky-tonk angels caught up with the western swing music originated by Bob Wills and the Texas Playboys. Those who flocked to Cain's forgot about their troubles to the rhythms of "Take Me Back to Tulsa," "Ida Red," "San Antonio Rose," "Osage Stomp," and "Faded Love."

Through most of the 1930s and 1940s, Wills and his band kept folks coming to Cain's, where there were daily radio broadcasts over KVOO — the fifty-thousand-watt, clear-channel "Voice of Oklahoma" — and overflow dances every Thursday and Saturday night. Legend has it that thousands of couples married thanks to Cain's and the haunting music of Wills and the Playboys.

On May 19, 1941, Wills himself met his future wife — a young lady named Betty Anderson, from nearby Sapulpa — during a dance at Cain's. Betty went to the bandstand to request a tune. She was so captivated by the smiling bandleader that she forgot her original request and asked Wills to play "You Are My Sunshine," a hit song he and Tex Ritter had introduced in the motion picture *Take Me Back to Oklahoma*. From that moment on, as far as Bob and Betty were concerned, "You Are My Sunshine" was *their song*.

In the late 1940s, after Bob moved to California, his brother Johnnie Lee Wills kept up the tradition of playing toe-tapping western swing at Cain's for many years. There were other owners, as well as a variety of bands, until 1976, when a young man named Larry Shaeffer bought the building. He booked rock and rollers, including the Pretenders and the Sex Pistols, but deep within his heart, Shaeffer knew Cain's was still a shrine to western swing. He was always glad when Ray Bensen and Asleep at the Wheel, lively Texans in the Wills tradition, returned to play at Cain's. When the new generation of musicians came to Tulsa, Shaeffer watched them enter the building with reverence. He realized they felt the ghosts there.

As rock bands began to gravitate toward larger venues such as big city arenas and Shaeffer approached his mid-forties, he decided it was time to sell Cain's and move on. One evening, potential buyers were invited to inspect the property on North Main. They peeked inside the ticket booth, ran their hands down the long bar, and sat on a sofa where it is said Hank Williams once passed out before he had a chance to play his second show. A real estate agent asked Shaeffer to give them a history of the place. As he stood before them on the dance floor, Shaeffer told many of the stories he knew of the bad and the good times, of bootleggers and brawls, of swaying lovers, and of a fiddle player from Turkey, Texas, whose music was heaven-sent.

When Shaeffer finished talking, his eyes were filled with tears. He looked at the people before him and saw that many of them also had been moved. Shaeffer knew then that he could not sell Cain's. On the walls hung the portraits and photographs of Bob Wills, his brothers Johnnie Lee and Luther, Hank Williams, Ernest Tubb, Tennessee Ernie Ford, Gene Autry, and Leon McAuliffe.

The ghosts had worked their magic.

For those of us who love country western music, Cain's is our Carnegie Hall.

— Red Steagall
Still Swingin': The History of Bob Wills and Western Swing Music

California, Here I Come

Popular song that first became a national hit in 1924.

■

All roads lead to California. We know whereof we speak because we have taken a few of them ourselves.

Throughout the history of the West, hordes of people poured into this land that inspired dreams. California attracted Native American tribes who were eventually slaughtered and forced into slavery, Portuguese mariners and English sailors, Spanish explorers looking for the legendary city called El Dorado, Russian fur trappers, Mexican and Anglo settlers, wagon trains loaded with pioneers such as the ill-fated Donner party, gold-rush hunters called forty-niners, Okies and dust bowl migrants, and so many others.

The Camino Real, Butterfield's Overland Mail, the Pony Express, the transcontinental railroad, and Route 66 all wound their way to the golden land on the Pacific shore. As California evolved under a dozen different flags, the waves of newcomers became as predictable as the fabled swallows that return each year to the mission at San Juan Capistrano.

Some people came seeking wealth from the vast store of natural resources. Others wanted to find fame and fortune in the movies, or were interested in basking in the state's enviable climate and landscapes. All were looking for the good life that California has always promised. Whether they were American Indian, Mexican, or Japanese, they all became not just the residents of a large state but — as O. Henry put it — a *race* of people known as Californians.

In the 1960s, more than 110 years after California became a state, many members of that race of people undoubtedly chose "California Dreamin' " — written by John Phillips and Michelle Phillips and recorded by the Mamas and the Papas in 1965 — as their new theme song. But time was not very kind to California. Promises the state once had offered to people were not always kept. Natural and man-made disasters also took a toll. Big cities — especially Los Angeles — became shrouded in smog and crime. A maze of concrete freeways and superhighways crisscrossed the land. The golden shine became tarnished.

Perhaps Guy Clark's soulful tune "L.A. Freeway" rings truer than most when it comes to what has happened to California. In the song, Clark laments that if he can "just get off of that L.A. Freeway without gettin' killed or caught, then I'll be down the road in a cloud of smoke to some land that I bought...."

Call of the Wild

A classic novel that will be read as long as little boys and girls exist, written by adventurer-author Jack London, pen name of John Griffith, 1876-1916. The book tells the story of Buck, a dog stolen from his home and thrown into the merciless life of the Klondike to endure hardship, bitter cold, and the savage lawlessness of men and beasts. London's story became the subject of feature films, including a 1935 version starring Clark Gable and Loretta Young.

Also, a phrase used to describe those voices that cry out to some people who dare to embrace the natural life of the American West.

■

From the deserts of the Southwest to the Rocky Mountains, from the high plains and prairies to the forests of the Pacific Northwest dwells an array of mammals, birds, reptiles, and insects that all of us have come to know — pronghorns, elk, mule deer, cougars, bobcats, porcupines, beavers, chipmunks, bighorn sheep, badgers, bats, javelinas, Inca doves, hawks, tortoises, tarantulas, and scorpions.

In our journeys across the West, we learned to value even the sometimes pesty prairie dogs and jackrabbits. We respect the Gila monster, a sluggish desert dweller and the lone poisonous lizard in the United States, and the rattlesnakes that control the rodent population. The horned toad, that spunky little sun worshiper, and the speedy roadrunner, often called the *paisano* (Spanish for "fellow countryman"), are two more critters of the West that enjoy a special place in our hearts. These creatures are some of our best teachers and friends.

"I should probably have been a wiser and better informed man had I spent more time out with the grasshoppers, horned toads, and coyotes," mused J. Frank Dobie in 1942. Like the famed Texas writer, we too are well aware of the link between humans and the entire cast of creatures that always have played important roles in the history, culture, and mythology of the American West. There are times when we wish we were like Buck, the dog in London's story, and could answer our own call of the wild.

Cow Towns

Sometimes called "cattle towns" by western-history snobs, a necklace of Kansas prairie hamlets that mushroomed along railroad lines during the boom days of the great cattle drives from Texas. Later, when the cattle drives had ended, *cow towns* referred to commercial centers in cattle country. Today, with the possible exception of Fort Worth, Texas — proud of its cow-town image — the term is used in a derogatory sense to describe a small, unsophisticated burg.

▪

Thanks to Saturday matinées and countless treks across the Land of Oz, we've visited just about every cow town Kansas has to offer. The drovers, soiled doves, gamblers, and old-time peace officers are gone, but the tales of the Kansas cow towns stubbornly persist. When the beef trade boomed, Newton, Ellsworth, Wichita, Hunnewell, Hays City, Caldwell, and so many others each had their heyday. But out of the pack, our two favorites are Abilene, incorporated in 1869, and Dodge City, a railhead on the Arkansas River.

▪

No one left in Abilene can recall those fleeting but colorful years when this town, 150 miles due west of Kansas City, was a wild and woolly haven for weary drovers and thirsty cowboys looking for relief after weeks of driving half-wild longhorn steers from Texas.

One of the earliest of a slew of Kansas cow towns (Baxter Springs, on Route 66, boasts of being "the first cow town in Kansas"), Abilene was the original terminus of the famous Chisholm Trail. James Butler "Wild Bill" Hickok, packing a pair of pearl-handled pistols, acted as town marshal for eight months in 1871. While there, Wild Bill gunned down two people, one of them a policeman. Twenty years later, the infant Dwight D. Eisenhower moved to Abilene with his family and grew up as the product of a sternly religious home.

During its boom years as a cow town, a *New York Tribune* reporter described Abilene as a "seething cauldron of vice and depravity." Times have changed. Today's Abilene — surrounded by wheat fields and site of the Greyhound Hall of Fame — serves as the final resting place for Ike and his wife, Mamie.

▪

Even though some western buffs prefer to call it the "queen of the cow towns," it should be pointed out that from its very beginnings in the early 1870s, Dodge City also was notorious as both the "wickedest little city in the world" and the "beautiful bibulous Babylon of the frontier."

It was commonly said about Dodge that a cowboy could break all the Ten Commandments in a single night, die with his boots on, and be laid to rest on Boot Hill the following morning. Not even the likes of Wyatt Earp, Doc Holliday, Bat Masterson, or Bill Tilghman could quite tame this Gomorrah of the Plains. It stands to reason, because except for "Uncle Billy" Tilghman, most of Dodge City's lawmen were themselves a bit tainted and tended to walk the shady side of those dusty streets.

It took television to bring justice to Dodge City. Each week for two decades, from 1955 to 1975, Marshal Matt Dillon rode into our living rooms along with his Dodge City cohorts, Miss Kitty Russell, owner of the Longbranch Saloon; Deputy Chester Goode (later replaced by Festus Haggen); and "Doc" Galen Adams. Twenty-six actors auditioned for the starring role of Matt Dillon, including

William Conrad, who had the role on radio, and Raymond Burr, but James Arness, a John Wayne protégé, won out.

Gunsmoke became the longest running western series in television history. Along with the popular *The Life and Legend of Wyatt Earp*, it is credited with having created the 1950s bonanza of TV westerns. Even "Duke" Wayne himself loved how Matt Dillon and his pals took care of things in lawless Dodge City. "I'm here to tell you about a Western … best thing of its kind that's come along," Wayne told America when introducing the premier episode of *Gunsmoke* on September 10, 1955. "It's honest. It's adult. It's realistic."

Reruns of old *Gunsmoke* episodes sometimes flash on the television screen at odd hours. They help to keep alive the tales of life in Dodge — hometown of Dennis Hopper, the original "Easy Rider," site of the Boot Hill Museum, and a town that still listens for the call of songdogs on the Kansas wind.

DFW

Common abbreviation for Dallas/Fort Worth International Airport, a major hub for the West located midway between Dallas and Fort Worth. When it opened in January 1974, DFW covered more than twenty-eight square miles, making it the nation's largest operating airport.

▪

A long time ago, when folks wished to escape the law, bad debts, or just wanted a new lease on life, they oftentimes packed up their belongings and carved *G.T.T.* in the bark of a shade tree, or left those three initials on a sign tacked to the front door of the house they were leaving behind. *G.T.T.* meant only one thing — *Gone to Texas*. Pretty soon that big, brash state became synonymous with getting a fresh start.

No one hangs out those kind of signs or defaces trees in that way anymore, but Texas still attracts plenty of newcomers. Instead of just being *G.T.T.*, most of those searching for greener pastures have in mind a particular city such as Houston, Austin, or San Antonio. Many of them choose to settle in Dallas or Fort Worth, or they opt for one of the bedroom communities spread between the two cities, now known simply as the Metroplex.

Although a majority of Texans believe that Dallas' true arch competitor is Houston — the state's largest city, 240 miles to the south — the rivalry between Dallas and neighboring Fort Worth cannot be ignored. Only thirty-three miles separate the two cities, but as John Gunther wrote, there "is a chasm practically as definitive as the Continental Divide." In plain old Texas English, Dallas and Fort Worth are *different*. They are as different from each other as a tuxedo and a pair of Levi's, as dissimilar as beefsteak and quiche, as distinct as tequila and soda pop.

People in Dallas believe their fair city is where the East ends, and the citizens of Fort Worth know full well that they live "Where the West Begins" — as proclaimed daily on the masthead of the *Fort Worth Star-Telegram.*

Both cities conjure up a whirlwind of images.

Founded on the banks of the Trinity River in 1841 by European immigrants who hoped to establish a social utopia in the wilderness, Dallas has become a frenzied skyline of steel, glass, and lights where big money talks and the nouveau riche rule. Anything even resembling an aristocracy is rooted only as far back as the 1930s, when Dallas got lucky as the prosperous East Texas oil patch made the city a banking haven and a southwestern center for manufacturing and fashion. But Dallas is more than the wheeler-dealer stereotype of the "Big D," as portrayed by the dysfunctional Ewing family rollicking on their Southfork Ranch in the old television series named after the city.

Dallas is:

▪ Coiffured Highland Park dowagers dripping in furs and jewels as they sip afternoon tea in the opulent Louis XIV lobby of the Adolphus Hotel, the grand Baroque structure built by beer baron Adolphus Busch in 1912.

▪ Budding designers who live by the adage, "If it doesn't sell in Dallas, it won't sell," headed off to the busy fashion market with Texas-sized hangovers after a night of partying in Deep Ellum, a district of renovated warehouses and garages.

▪ A weary salesman with more air miles under his belt than a dozen flying aces, glancing for the thousandth time at the big bronze statue of a Texas Ranger caught in perpetual midstride in the lobby of Love Field.

▪ Generations of loyal shoppers drawn to the original Neiman Marcus, the celebrated retail store — famous for its international Fortnights, Christmas catalog, and customer service — that has dressed Dallas and pampered the rich and famous since 1907.

▪ A covey of former Dallas Cowboy cheerleaders — platinum blonde hair sprayed stiff as meringue — wining and dining the night away with their plastic-surgeon husbands at the Mansion on Turtle Creek, an expensive restaurant with an eclectic menu, where reservations must be made weeks in advance.

▪ A young woman who had not yet been born on November 22, 1963, poring over the memory books where visitors record personal thoughts at the Sixth Floor, a permanent exhibition which examines the life, death, and lasting legacy of John F. Kennedy, in the old Texas School Book Depository overlooking Dealey Plaza.

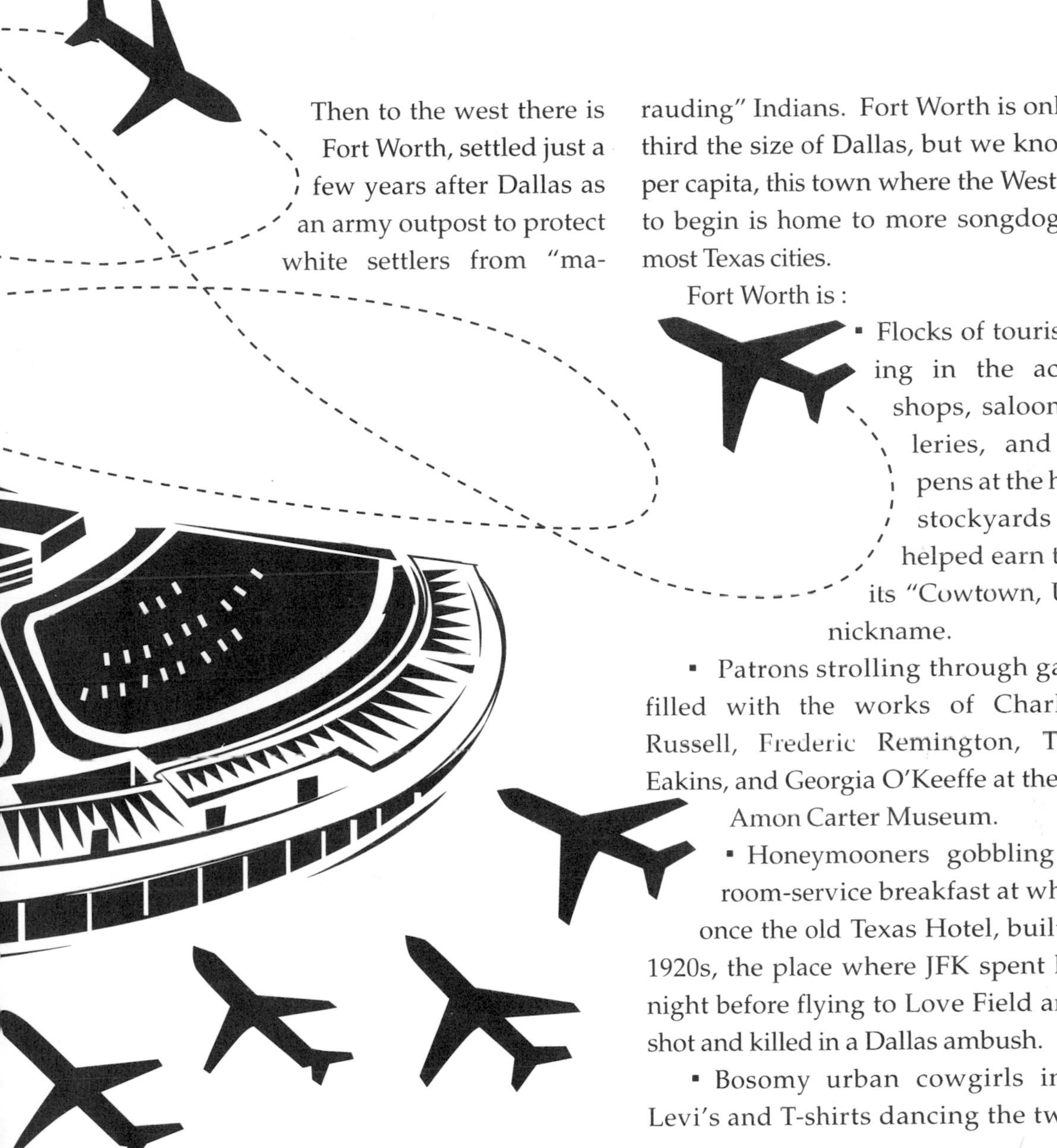

Then to the west there is Fort Worth, settled just a few years after Dallas as an army outpost to protect white settlers from "marauding" Indians. Fort Worth is only one-third the size of Dallas, but we know that per capita, this town where the West is said to begin is home to more songdogs than most Texas cities.

Fort Worth is :

- Flocks of tourists taking in the acres of shops, saloons, galleries, and cattle pens at the historic stockyards that helped earn the city its "Cowtown, U.S.A." nickname.
- Patrons strolling through galleries filled with the works of Charles M. Russell, Frederic Remington, Thomas Eakins, and Georgia O'Keeffe at the famed Amon Carter Museum.
- Honeymooners gobbling down room-service breakfast at what was once the old Texas Hotel, built in the 1920s, the place where JFK spent his last night before flying to Love Field and was shot and killed in a Dallas ambush.
- Bosomy urban cowgirls in snug Levi's and T-shirts dancing the two-step

with their best beaus at Billy Bob's Texas, an old cattle barn made over into the world's largest honky-tonk.

▪ A bowlegged Texan with crow's-feet eyes taking his grandson to M.L. Leddy's Western Store for a pair of handcrafted boots that would have made "Daddy Joe" Justin green with envy.

▪ Office workers on lunch break perusing their latest find from Barber's Book Store ("fine old books since 1925") while school kids parade through fountains, cascades, and bubbling pools at the downtown water garden.

Unfortunately, there is more to the Metroplex than Dallas and Fort Worth. In the expanse between the two cities and surrounding them are countless industrial sites, shopping malls, and look-alike suburbs. Called the "Mid Cities," these homogenized communities with names such as Addison, Arlington, Carrollton, Farmers Branch, Garland, Granbury, Grand Prairie, Grapevine, Irving, McKinney, Mesquite, Plano, and Richardson continue to grow like fungi, feeding off the two larger cities that give them life. In that limbo land of anonymous suburban sprawl that has forever linked Dallas and Fort Worth is a cookie-cutter theme amusement park called Six Flags over Texas, a big-league baseball park, and a football stadium for the Dallas Cowboys, called by some people "America's team."

And there is DFW. This international airport of endless tarmacs, terminals, and parking lots, automated electric cars, and maze of looping roads and runways is an industry in itself. For thousands and thousands of travelers, it is the first and only impression they have of Texas. Sadly, it also stands as a symbol of two very distinctive cities that will never be the same. Dallas and Fort Worth should quit worrying about Houston and stop calling each other names. Perhaps they are not the real rivals after all. Maybe their true enemy has become that huge slice of generic America that steadily creeps in and, with each tick of the clock, steals away more of their identity.

Devil's Rope

When barbed wire first appeared in the 1870s, this derogatory name was used by religious groups and animal-rights activists who considered the earliest versions cruel and vicious because the razor-sharp barbs cut so many cattle, horses, and men. A good many spirited cowboys and veteran cattle drovers also cursed the wire. They not only called it *devil's rope* but also *devil's hatband* and *devil's necklace* because they hated to see their wide-open rangeland fenced. Most intelligent historians agree that along with windmills and trains, the advent of barbed-wire fencing did more to tame the West than anything else, including the six-gun.

■

In the picturesque Texas panhandle town called McLean, where tumbleweeds roll down the streets and old-timers gather at the Cowboy Drive-in Cafe to eat chili burgers and swap lies, an old brick and masonry building that used to house a brassière factory has been transformed into the Devil's Rope Museum — a monument to barbed wire that has no equal. Although barbed-wire enthusiasts at La Crosse, Kansas, burst with pride that their small town is the self-appointed barbed-wire capital, even they have to admit that McLean's museum houses the largest collection of barbed wire in the world.

It is fitting that a Texas town in cattle country should be the site of the most examples of the many types of barbed wire ever assembled under one roof. After all, it was Texas where, by the late 1870s, those first purveyors of devil's rope had to persuade a legion of reluctant cowboys and cattlemen whose favorite battle cry was no longer "Remember the Alamo" but "Don't fence me in."

A major proponent in the barbed-wire manufacturers' struggle to win over reluctant Texans was a brash young salesman from Illinois named John Warne Gates. He was given the formidable task of selling Lone Star State cowboys on the merits of devil's rope.

A natural-born gambler, Gates had earned a colorful nickname during a train trip when he placed huge wagers with fellow salesman on the speed of raindrops sliding down the window of the Pullman car. The betting was fast and furious throughout the rainstorm, with stakes sometimes as much as a thousand dollars on each drop of rain. Gates never flinched. By the time the train stopped, he had acquired a pile of money and the moniker "Bet-a-Million."

When twenty-one-year-old Gates hit San Antonio in 1876, he knew he had his work cut out for him. He picked up his drummer's satchel and took to the ranch roads, trying his best to sell rolls of the despised wire that many people believed had to be the work of Satan himself. Try as he might, Gates met with slim success. Not only were sales slow, but most ranchers snorted that whoever came up with the notion of "bob wire" should have a bunch of the prickly stuff wrapped around him in a ball, and that ball should be rolled straight into hell.

Then one evening after he watched a shrewd peddler sell patent medicine as if it were going out of style, Gates found the solution he needed. If an old rascal snake-oil quack could win over Texans, so could Gates. He would use the same approach, putting on a regular show for the citizens of San Antonio and the ranchers who came to buy supplies and take in the city's sights.

Gates got permission from local officials to erect a sturdy corral on the Military Plaza, right on the spot where San Antonio's City Hall would stand later. Instead of a wooden enclosure, Gates had his crews build an eight-strand barbed-wire fence. Then he issued his famous challenge: "This is the finest fence in the world. Light as air. Stronger than whiskey. Cheaper than dirt. All steel, and miles long. The cattle ain't been born that can get through it. Bring on your steers, gentlemen!"

There are as many different accounts of what happened next as there are chili parlors in San Antonio. The popular version is that Gates had some cowboys drive a couple of dozen of the meanest longhorns alive into the wire corral and turn them loose. The half-wild steers, seeing nothing between them and freedom but a few strands of wire, charged the fence. They were repulsed quickly by the barbs. Time and again, the longhorns snorted and pawed the dust and made runs at the fence, only to be turned back. Pretty soon, the cattle gave up and settled down. The barbed wire had held. The audience that had gathered in the plaza stopped laughing, and their guffaws turned to cheers.

It is said that by sundown, "Bet-a-Million" Gates had sold hundreds of miles of barbed wire. Devil's rope was an idea whose time had come.

Disneyland

Opened in Anaheim, California, in July 1955, and in the opinion of many, still the world's best amusement park.

■

Disneyland was the brainchild of Walter Elias Disney, known simply as Walt. A school dropout who endured his father's harsh beatings, Disney served as an ambulance driver in France during World War I. He went on to work as a commercial artist in Kansas City before moving west to Hollywood in the early 1920s to make animated movies.

A diehard Republican, Disney hired few minorities and became known as one of the leading Hollywood figures obsessed with ferreting out Communists in the motion-picture industry. Disney, along with other conservative California business tycoons, persuaded Ronald Reagan to give up his mediocre acting career and enter the political arena. Disney especially took a liking to Reagan after the future president became a star witness fingering Communists for congressional investigators.

Beyond Walt's right-wing political activities and before his death in 1966, the studio which bears his name had given us cartoon character notables such as Mickey

Mouse, Donald Duck, Pluto, and Goofy, and the classic films *Snow White and the Seven Dwarfs, Pinocchio, Fantasia,* and *Cinderella*. Walt and his troops were also responsible for a bevy of wholesome action movies and wildlife documentaries, the now legendary *Mickey Mouse Club*, and a revival of interest in crusty frontiersman Davy Crockett.

But the seventy-six-acre dream park that Disney carved out of southern California orange groves gave all of us a chance to do more than just gawk at the big screen and boob tube with our mouse ears and coonskin caps in place. It was a perfect world free of disorder, poverty, violent fathers, and Communists — an idyllic controlled environment in which unpleasant memories could be replaced by sweet dreams. Disney invited us to enter the seven theme areas in his park and become part of the action. We could take an exciting jungle cruise through Adventureland, board a raft bound for rustic Tom Sawyer Island in Frontierland, or step into Fantasyland and see "Flying Dumbos" and attend the "Mad Tea Party." We brushed shoulders with Wild West figures, cartoon characters, and other celluloid heroes who came to life in the Magic Kingdom.

Dwarfed by the sprawling Walt Disney World, which opened in Florida in 1971, Disneyland remains the prototype for escapism. It's neat, it's clean, and all the bullets are blanks. If only the "happiest place on earth" had been there when Billy the Kid was looking for a place to hide!

As Walt Disney unveiled his uniquely American creation, Disneyland, he also exposed the unbridled optimism in technological progress, industrial expansion, and romantic saga that so marked Anglo-American thinking in the twentieth-century American West. . . . Disney's fantasies, as exemplified in Disneyland, were characteristic of an entire migrant generation who made their way to California and other parts of the West in the first half of the twentieth century. . . . Disneyland also represented a frustration with the growing sprawl and diverse population of the urban West and the associated problems of traffic congestion, pollution, overcrowding, and alienation after World War II. Disney saw his park as a leisurely retreat from that civic confusion as well as a platform to show what life in a metropolis could be like if planned correctly.

— *The Oxford History of the American West*

The Duke

Popular nickname for John Wayne, 1907-1979. Born Marion Michael Morrison in Winterset, Iowa, Wayne was raised in California, where he developed into a football star and worked part time as a laborer and prop boy in Hollywood. Early on, he developed a close relationship with film director John Ford, who played a decisive part in shaping Wayne into a motion picture legend. By 1928, Wayne — billed as Duke Morrison — was cast as a bit player in some of Ford's films. In 1930, he received his big break when Ford saw to it that director Raoul Walsh cast the strapping Wayne as the lead in *The Big Trail*. Throughout his screen career of more than forty years, Wayne appeared in about 250 films, including such western classics as *Stagecoach, Red River, She Wore a Yellow Ribbon, The Searchers*, and *The Horse Soldiers*.

■

We figured out the John Wayne mystique one quiet afternoon at the National Cowboy Hall of Fame in Oklahoma City. It was not during a lecture about Wayne and his films, or in something we found in a thick tome chronicling his life. Our revelation came on the lower level, not far from the Chapel of Hats, where a bunch of old cowboy hats hangs in tribute to the movie stars and deceased museum trustees who once wore them.

Nearby, we encountered the John Wayne Gallery, featuring part of the movie star's personal collection of bronzes and paintings, guns, knives, movie posters, saddles, and other memorabilia. Among the items in the rather eclectic display, we saw the Colt pistol Wayne had used in his famous shoot-out scene with the bad guys in *True Grit*, the film that earned him an Academy Award for playing one-eyed lawman Rooster Cogburn.

We worked our way through a dark passageway. Along the walls, lighted grottoes held some of the kachina dolls and other curiosities the movie star had donated to the Hall of Fame just weeks before his death. At the end of the corridor was a small room where the best John Wayne film moments were shown perpetually on video. The floor and walls, covered with thick carpeting, gave viewers the sensation of being in a protective cocoon while they witnessed Wayne take on "hostile Indians" and the vilest of outlaws. Wayne's distinctive voice, tempered by a lifetime of cigarettes and whiskey and filled with bravado, growled in the background.

Two middle-aged women joined us and the kachinas. Their big pink plastic hair rollers were covered with brightly colored synthetic scarves. Every piece of clothing they wore was adorned with pseudo designer labels and American flags. The smell of cigarette smoke rose from their windbreakers, and they chewed wads of gum in unison. These women were pure, red-blooded Americans. They were just exactly the kind of folks that John Wayne had fought for on the big screen for so many years. The man who was so much bigger than actual life and who became the epitome of the gung-ho superpatriot would have loved these two ladies.

Moving with obvious reverence and awe, as though they were visiting a sacred place, the pair of women — who dared to communicate only in the muted whispers usually reserved for church — may as well have been genuflecting before each of the displays.

"Just think, Doris," one of the women whispered loud enough for us to hear, "this is the closest we'll ever get to 'the Duke.' "

Her friend, absolutely speechless, nodded in agreement.

They looked into each other's faces before continuing toward John Wayne's voice. It was too shadowy to see, but we imagined that tears were welling in their eyes.

Eagles

In the American West there are two types of raptors, or birds of prey, known as eagles — the bald eagle, America's national bird, and the larger golden eagle. Also, the name of a group of musicians and singers who first rose to popularity in the 1970s with their "country-rock" music.

▪

No matter if it's a bright winter morning on the Arkansas River, out among the mesas and mountains of the Southwest, or along a logger's road on the Olympic Peninsula, we never grow weary of watching the comings and goings of eagles, be they the bald or the golden variety.

We have forged friendships with men and women from throughout the West who have devoted themselves and their energies to protecting these huge birds.

There was Shawn Ogburn and the Raptor Preservation Fund, a grass-roots group we encountered on the brink of the Texas Hill Country. Battling in behalf of all birds of prey, these preservationists used as their symbol a golden eagle that had been left permanently disabled by some trigger-happy person.

We also cheered when John Elliott, a former pro football star, returned to his native Texas to become a county sheriff and halt a wholesale slaughter of golden eagles, erroneously blamed for feasting on lambs and kid goats. The lawman took head-on some influential politicians and ranchers who had financed the helicopter crew that shot seventy eagles from the skies. He did not rest until the culprits were brought to justice.

In Oklahoma, we observed a confederacy of unabashed eagle lovers at the George Miksch Sutton Avian Research Center and its ongoing efforts to replenish dwindling populations of bald eagles throughout the country and educate the public about the birds' importance. One of the participants told us that he considered eagles works of art that never can be replaced. When an eagle was killed, it was just like someone slashing a Rembrandt, he said.

Despite our continued involvement with eagles and the people and groups who champion them, there are eagles of yet another feather we also revere.

Identified with the California scene even though most of the members came from small towns in the heartland, the Eagles and their music brought us back to nature as we moseyed down the spectacular Pacific coast, raced across the high plains, or cruised beneath a desert moon. We remain unabashed fans. Whenever we hear "Take It to the Limit," "Tequila Sunrise," " Hotel California," "Take It Easy," "Lyin' Eyes," "The Best of My Love," or "Witchy Woman," a flood of pleasant memories engulfs us. Like the "Desperado" they sing of, we always come to our senses whenever the Eagles take flight.

Easy Rider

A low-budget blockbuster, this escapist motion picture of drugs, travel, and counterculture characters premiered in July 1969. It starred Dennis Hopper, the film's director, as "Billy the Kid," and Peter Fonda, the film's producer, as "Captain America." It also featured Jack Nicholson as a drunken civil-rights attorney. Much more than a biker odyssey, this phenomenally successful film helped to define its time and captured the true feelings of disenfranchised American youths in the late 1960s.

▪

Inspired by Jack Kerouac and his powerful novel of youth adrift that had already turned on a whole generation before us, we stayed out on the open roads of the West for much of the summer of 1969. It was time well spent. The Age of Aquarius was dawning, and we wanted to assist with the birth.

It proved to be a pivotal moment not only for us but for the entire nation. That summer of '69 brought Hurricane Camille, the rise of the Miracle Mets, and men on the moon. While Richard M. Nixon and his zany sidekick, Spiro Agnew, championed their "silent majority," more death and destruction rained down in Vietnam. According to the Nielsen's, the best that television had to offer was *Rowan and Martin's Laugh-In*, *Gunsmoke*, and *Bonanza*. *Hee-Haw* and *The Brady Bunch* made their debuts. O.J. Simpson, the highest-paid football rookie of the year, reported to training camp to begin his professional career.

We learned new names that summer, such as Chappaquiddick and Mary Jo Kopechne, Neil Armstrong, Leno and Rosemary LaBianca, William Calley, and Max Yasgur, whose dairy farm near Bethel, New York, attracted 400,000 pilgrims — the "Woodstock Nation" — for three days of peace and music.

In early August, we found ourselves in California, along with loved ones and friends who shared our sense of adventure. Young and carefree, all of us agreed with Steppenwolf that as nature's true children, we were "Born To Be Wild." Short days past, our trail was still fresh from Saint Louis to Boulder through Wyoming and Salt Lake City to San Francisco. There for a few memorable days, we wore flowers in our hair, prowled the steep back streets and crowded boulevards, and discussed politics and the insanity of a

godless war over espresso lunches. Each evening, we sipped sweet wine, counted the cold Pacific stars, and fed driftwood and dreams into a beach fire that we were convinced would never burn out.

Then we entered the belly of the beast. We were there during the madness and mayhem of two muggy summer nights in L.A. when seven people — a pregnant actress named Sharon Tate and her friends, followed by a grocer and his wife — were butchered in an orgy of violence by psychotic misfits under the spell of the demonic Charles Manson. Arrests would not be made for several months. While a police dragnet searched for the bloodthirsty killers, some of us sought refuge from the insanity by twirling in Disney's giant teacups before returning to the sanctuary of the road. We found more comfort farther down the coast in a crumbling San Clemente hotel that echoed with the radio voices of Bob Dylan's "Lay Lady Lay" and Blood, Sweat and Tears singing "Spinning Wheels."

Inspired to streak down the freeways of southern California to the Mexican border, we flirted with danger on our own terms by rotating drivers and taking turns at the wheel in an automobile speeding way too fast. To celebrate survival, we entered Tijuana on foot and hitched a ride in the back of a pickup to the bullring by the sea. We took seats in the sun high above the dusty arena to witness a daily contest pitting the lithe matador against *el toro*. We already knew that by the close of that long afternoon, the brave bulls, as always, would lose.

We raced on, and never once looked in the rearview mirror. Taking different paths through the Mojave and across the sun-baked mountains of Arizona, we rendezvoused in the heart of Albuquerque and made our commitment to Santa Fe at the feet of a burning Zozobra. Finally, we zoomed south through Billy the Kid terrain to El Paso del Norte before splintering in differ-

ent directions like the fiery sparks of an exploding skyrocket.

Our "Easy Rider" summer ended soon enough, with the voices of Woodstock — Hendrix, Joplin, Havens, Hardin, Jefferson Airplane, Creedence Clearwater Revival, and all the others from that August — still echoing in our thoughts. But more changes were in the wind, including the specter of violence and death.

Within weeks, we learned the truth about the massacre twenty months before of hundreds of innocents at a hamlet called My Lai. In Washington, thousands of peaceful protesters demanded an end to the hideous war in Vietnam. Just months after Woodstock, we shuddered when the Rolling Stones' free concert at a speedway near San Francisco turned into what became known as the Altamont Death Festival. As the Stones sang "Sympathy for the Devil," a wild posse of Hell's Angels, hired by the band as security guards for five hundred dollars' worth of beer, clubbed bystanders with pool cues and stabbed and kicked to death a young man who dared to approach the stage.

By that autumn, the time of *Midnight Cowboy* and the quiet passing of Kerouac, one of us lived in the upper stories of an old tavern called the Last Chance Saloon, not far from the west bank of the Mississippi. The other of our duo had moved to Santa Fe to prepare for the migration of our Spinners that would take place by year's end. As we had done before and would continue to do, we had come full circle.

We are stardust,
We are golden,
And we've got to get ourselves
Back to the garden.

— Joni Mitchell
"Woodstock," 1969

El Paso del Norte

Alvar Núñez Cabeza de Vaca came upon the "Pass to the North" in 1536, almost a century before the establishment of Plymouth and Jamestown. Spanish conquistadores, Indian tribes, traders, soldiers, and adventurers funneled through the pass, known as the lowest in the Rocky Mountains. Modern El Paso remains an important border crossing and port of entry connected by bridges over the Rio Grande to the state of Chihuahua and Ciudad Juárez, one of the largest cities in Mexico.

▪

El Paso was never our favorite place to be in March — too many memories. That's when the wind was likely to come howling up out of Chihuahua and off the New Mexican desert, leaving the city sandblasted and feeling even more cut off from the rest of the world than it really is. When the heavens turned dark yellow, people tried to escape the gritty blast. Men and boys turned up their collars, women wrapped their heads in scarves, and little girls in Loretto Academy uniform skirts hunkered down at bus stops to shield bare legs from the stinging sand. Soldiers training at Fort Bliss grew more homesick than ever.

One of us was born and raised in El Paso, and witnessed annual sandstorms that were as much a part of the city's way of life back then as the Sun Bowl parade, trips to Tony Lama's original shop for new boots to wear to the rodeo, and teenage forays across the river to toss back tequilas at the Kentucky Club or sip forbidden cocktails in mariachi bars.

▪

My father's family was Irish. The day he was born in El Paso — May 7, 1911 — last-minute peace negotiations broke down across town between delegates of the crumbling regime of the ruthless Mexican President Porfirio Díaz and the insurgent provisional president, Francisco Madero. Pancho Villa had already arrived in Juárez from the south leading his band of bold rebel soldiers, with their great mustaches, sombreros, and bandoliers of cartridges crisscrossed on their chests.

The following day, the first major battle of the long, bloody Mexican Revolution erupted across the Rio Grande in the streets of Juárez. El Pasoans flocked to the riverbanks, stood on railroad boxcars, or peered with spyglasses from the city's heights to watch the battle unfold. Some citizens tossed candies and cookies across the river to the revolutionaries, while others broke out their Kodaks to capture images of history in the making. Young rebels who saw the flashes of sun glint on the cameras smiled and waved.

Long after the guns fell silent, my family was still in El Paso. My father ventured away from time to time, but he was always drawn back. Maybe the old adage is true — "If you wear out one pair of shoes in El Paso, you will never leave." My father wore out many pairs. He is buried not far from the border. Next to him rests my Danish mother, and nearby are the graves of her parents and so many of my father's Irish kinfolk.

Both of his sisters also remained in El Paso. One died very young, and the other one married into another Irish family rooted deep in the El Paso soil. They were building contractors, and their work stretched from the border to the state capital. They also kept strong ties to the Catholic Church. When one of the old patriarchs of the family was ready to die, it was noted that he had done so much for his Mother Church that the archbishop himself came, in full regalia, with his entourage. He stood at the deathbed and, before administering last rites, he declared the old Irishman, with seven grown children, an honorary Jesuit.

I was not surprised that the Irish side of my family got along so well in a place dominated by Hispanics. I knew that the Irish and the Mexicans have always been simpático. Back during the war of 1846-48 when the United States invaded Mexico, some of the soldiers from north of the border hailed from the Old Sod. Army recruiters grabbed the Irish lads straight off the boats they had boarded in Ireland to escape the potato famine. Once the fledgling soldiers, known as the Saint Patrick Battalion, were engaged in combat and witnessed the gringo atrocities being leveled against the Mexicans, the Irishmen became disillusioned. They defected to the Mexican army to fight alongside brethren united with them in a common faith and lifestyle. The price they paid was steep. After a bloody battle in which most were killed, the survivors of the Saint Patrick Battalion were hanged by the U.S. Army from a makeshift gallows within sight of the Mexican fortress of Chapultepec.

▪

Like the gathering of old Irish clans, now and then we rendezvous in El Paso with family and friends. At one get-together, despite warnings that thieves sometimes operated in the area, four of us decided to make a pilgrimage to the top of Mount Cristo Rey.

Three miles from downtown El Paso, the 4,576-foot peak marks the spot where two nations — the United States and Mexico — and three states — Texas, New Mexico, and Chihuahua — merge. At the summit stands a thirty-three-and-a-half-foot statue of Christ the King, one foot taller than the Christ of the Andes between Argentina and Chile. Instead of pausing like pious pilgrims at each of the fourteen stations of the cross along the way, we were determined to run up the steep two-mile trail.

Fresh and fit, the four of us — two men and two women — began our ascent. Soon we found our own rhythms apart from one another, and became lost in thought. One at a time, we rounded a sharp turn and came upon several young Mexican men sitting on rocks along the edge of the trail. They didn't respond to our smiles or greetings, but only stared as we moved past them. Farther ahead, we encountered more of them, only this time, we noticed that several had long knives tucked into their belts or carried wooden clubs. Mostly teenagers, they had the look of bandits. More began to appear among the boulders. By the time each of us reached the crest of the mountain, our foursome was glad to be reunited.

As we caught our breath, we noticed that the dozen or so Mexicans we had passed on the trail had followed us to the top. We were left with a sinking feeling as they slowly closed in around us.

Suddenly one of our friends had an idea. A skilled photographer, he almost always carried a camera with him, and this day was no exception. In a bandanna tied to his running shorts was a new Polaroid and some film. He quickly unwrapped the camera, gave us a wink, and turned to face the approaching gang. With smiles, we too turned toward the Mexican boys and gestured for them to join us at the base of the huge Cordova cream limestone Christ. Startled by our friendliness but curious, the gang followed along. We arranged them in orderly rows for a group portrait, making sure the most ominous looking of the bunch — the apparent leader — was given a prominent place in the front row. We joined their ranks, and like victorious athletes with arms on one another's shoulders, everyone grinned for the camera as our friend shot picture after picture. It was a scene reminiscent of 1911, when the revolution raged and a camera lens united two nations.

When all the film was shot, the boys huddled around us, pleased with the Polaroid's quick results. We presented a half dozen portraits to the beaming ringleader, and quietly took our leave. As the four of us began our descent, breathing deep sighs of relief, the gang of boys broke into cheers and raised their fists in the air to salute us. All the way down the rocky path, we heard their voices echoing, bouncing from New Mexico to Texas and tumbling south into old Mexico.

Some may say it was the luck of the Irish, but we think not. Perhaps the ghosts of the Saint Patrick Battalion ran alongside us that day.

From the Faraway Nearby

An evocative phrase often used by renowned artist Georgia O'Keeffe to sign her letters from New Mexico to friends back east. Also, the title of a 1937 mystical O'Keeffe oil painting of an elk's skull and antlers hovering above snowcapped mountains at sunrise.

■

The first time we laid eyes on Georgia O'Keeffe was at a health-food store on one of the narrow avenues just a few blocks from the Santa Fe plaza. It was during the noon hour, and the small shop was busy with tourists and locals seeking pills, powders, pollens, and potions that help to fuel the economy of the health-conscious resort city.

We watched a woman quietly enter, walk straight to a shelf, and seize a jar of capsules, undoubtedly vitamins or some sort of natural remedy. It was Georgia O'Keeffe, one of the world's preeminent artists and a living icon of the West.

Her silvery hair was pulled back, and a striking woolen shawl covered her shoulders. Her hands — still as talented as they had been in decades past when photographed by the great Alfred Stieglitz — crowned a smooth wooden walking stick. Her eagle eyes, set in that familiar furrowed face, surveyed the milling crowd of browsers trying to make up their minds, and a long line of shoppers bearing armloads of goods waiting to pay. No one seemed to notice O'Keeffe.

After a moment of watching the hopeless scene before her, O'Keeffe lifted her walking stick and rapped it hard on the floor. The sharp sound rang like a pistol shot, and every head in the place turned toward her.

"I am Georgia O'Keeffe," she announced to a surprised throng of people who immediately recognized her. "I'm sorry, but you will all have to wait."

With that, Miss O'Keeffe strode directly to the cash register at the head of the line and quickly paid for her one item. Without another word, she turned and departed. Everyone watched as she entered a car with a driver waiting at the curb, and sped away.

That was a rare sighting of Miss O'Keeffe. During the many years she lived in northern New Mexico, she journeyed to Santa Fe for supplies and occasional meetings with a small circle of friends. She preferred the solitude and tranquility at the homes she kept in the village of Abiquiu and nearby Ghost Ranch.

Stories about the reclusive artist will live forever in the Chama River valley. One popular account is of a famous photographer who, after long negotiations, set up an appointment in Abiquiu to photograph Miss O'Keeffe in her artistic habitat. The photographer knocked on O'Keeffe's door only to find that the plainly dressed woman who answered was the legendary artist herself. The stunned man, who had assumed he would be greeted by a servant, could only manage to mutter that he had come to see Georgia O'Keeffe.

After peering at the photographer for what seemed to him an eternity, O'Keeffe turned her back to him and then turned around again.

"Now you've seen Georgia O'Keeffe — front and back," she reportedly said before shutting the door in his face.

The best O'Keeffe stories have not appeared in print or film. Perhaps it's better that way. These are vintage memories of Georgia O'Keeffe. These are the recollections of her Hispanic neighbors in Abiquiu who remember her not only as an acclaimed artist, but as an Anglo woman who chose to live, grow old, and die in their midst.

They are stories not just of O'Keeffe the visionary, who created striking images of their beloved landscape, but also remembrances of how the land and the elements nurtured a fellow villager as she went about her daily routine.

Generations of these New Mexicans became acquainted with O'Keeffe. Some knew her as a friend and confidante, others as an employer capable of throwing fits of frugality or demonstrating acts of generosity. No matter if they cooked for O'Keeffe, plastered her adobe walls, stretched her canvases, broke bread with her, or sold her canned goods at the local general store, they speak of O'Keeffe not as an icon but as a human being. They recall that she was a mortal, like them, who will forever remain part of that land she called "the faraway nearby."

Gateway Arch

The tallest monument in the United States and a symbol of the city of Saint Louis, the stainless-steel Arch soars 630 feet above the Mississippi River. Designed by famed architect Eero Saarinen and completed in 1965, this engineering feat commemorates the city's impact on westward expansion as the storied Gateway to the West.

▪

Established in 1764 by the French along the mighty Mississippi just below its confluence with the Missouri river, Saint Louis was named for Louis IX, patron saint of the reigning monarch of France, Louis XV. From its beginning, the city acted as a commercial center on the edge of the frontier, attracting merchants, steamboat captains, beer barons, and railroaders. It was also a jumping-off place for adventurers, fur trappers, soldiers, and sodbusters.

Citizens were proud that their city was a key crossroads and a leading industrial and transportation hub. As the nineteenth century drew to a close, Saint Louis — tempered by political upheaval, social conflict, cholera epidemics, and waterfront fires — emerged as one of the largest and most vibrant cities in the United States. Although it had been founded by the French and, for a time, was governed by the Spanish, Saint Louis became a melting pot of cultures and customs. The population swelled with waves of Germans, Italians, Irish, and African-Americans, all of whom left their distinctive marks. It often was said that the whole world passed through the old river city.

▪

We have both lived in Saint Louis, but one of us is a native.

My father was born in Saint Louis less than one year after the close of the

Louisiana Purchase Exposition of 1904 — revered by most historians as the greatest of all world's fairs. From my father and other family members, I was given an endless supply of stories of the city at its zenith. I learned of a household where German was spoken until the Great War interrupted. I heard about the idyllic "Meet Me in St. Louis" years of streetcar excursions and picnics at Tower Grove and Forest Park, and of seminary students sharing Sabbath dinners provided by neighborhood butcher shops and the vendors of the Soulard Market.

There were plenty of tales of a German-born great-grandfather who was one of the finest brickmasons in the city. Every single workday, he sent a hod carrier to Busch's brewery, with its huge copper vats and Clydesdale horses in leather and brass harnesses, to fetch a bucket of suds for washing down lunches of rye bread and limburger cheese.

My great-grandfather's crews laid the bricks that supported many of the tall church spires dotting the south side. Most were places of worship for the Saxon Lutherans and Rhineland Catholics, but sometimes the German bricklayers were called on to build a Baptist church. When that happened, it was said that my great-grandfather got a gleam in his eye as he ordered his men to be sure to splash some of their beer into that very, very dry Baptist mortar.

When we go home to Saint Louis, I like to drive through the old neighborhoods where my ancestors once lived and worked. Taverns continue to anchor most corners, and the distinctive aroma of cooking beer from Busch's old brewhouse permeates the air. Fresh vegetables, fruit, and spices are still sold at Soulard. All the churches — Lutheran, Catholic, and Baptist — stand ramrod straight, bound together by mortar laced with lager.

But if we really want to see Saint Louis, we drive out of the city. We go across the broad river to the Illinois bottomlands and visit the famed Cahokia Mounds.

Created by Native American people known as Mississippians beginning in about A.D. 700, these earthen mounds provide the ideal perspective for viewing the city. No bricks or mortar were used or required. The soil was dug by tools fashioned of wood, stone, or shell, and carried in baskets to the various mound locations. Originally there were more than 120 mounds. Many were destroyed centuries later by farmers and urban encroachment, but thankfully, the site finally was saved and will be preserved forever.

Rising in four terraces to a height of one hundred feet, Monks Mound dominates the site. It was named for French Trappist monks who lived there for a short time in the early 1800s and planted gardens and orchards on its terraces. The largest Indian mound north of Mexico, it was built in stages between A.D. 900 and 1200, and its base covers fourteen acres. The principal ruler of this once flourishing culture maintained a massive residence on the mound's summit, from which he governed his empire, conferred with other nobles, and conducted ceremonies.

Larger than the Great Pyramid of Giza, the flattopped mound offers a bird's-eye view of the Saint Louis skyline and the soaring Gateway Arch. That is why we went there one clear winter afternoon the day before New Year's Eve — the ideal time for contemplation and reflection.

We stood on Monk's Mound and pondered those people — as many as twenty thousand — who long before had lived in this sophisticated settlement covering more than six square miles, with homes, sweat lodges, and temples clustered around open plazas. We visualized the growing fields of corn, squash, and beans outside stockade walls, and the smoke rising from sacred fires. We gazed at the nearby Arch gleaming in the sunlight, and we recalled that Saint Louis was nicknamed "Mound City" because twenty-six mounds had been in the downtown area before the large numbers of white people arrived. What eventually became Saint Louis was actually a satellite village — a suburb — of the larger Cahokia settlement. By the time my father was born, almost all of those ancient mounds had been destroyed, replaced by red brick homes, civil buildings, churches, and warehouses.

On New Year's Eve — back on the west side of the great river — we gathered with hundreds of others in downtown Saint Louis to observe the close of the old year and the birth of the new in a celebration known simply as First Night. Six hours of festivity filled the downtown streets and avenues, transforming the area into a giant stage complete with costumed dancers, magicians, mimes, choral groups, jazz musicians, jugglers, storytellers, and poets.

Just before midnight, large snowflakes began to fall, as if on cue. Then, as the countdown came and ended, with the revelers breaking into cries of "Happy New Year!" a

cascade of fireworks erupted over the Mississippi. It was the most spectacular display we had ever seen, and it went on and on. We raced from the screaming pack of people and made our way toward the river. In front of one of the hotels, couples in fancy gowns and tuxedos left the ballrooms and champagne toasts and came outside to watch the colorful aerial show. We saw their steamy breath, and the lights flashing in their eyes.

The fireworks in the snowy skies reflected off the looking-glass buildings and the shiny steel skin of the Arch. We passed the Renaissance dome of the Old Courthouse, where slaves were once sold and where Dred Scott, an unknown black man, unsuccessfully sued for his freedom in 1847 in trials that helped to spark the Civil War. We looked to our right and saw the ballpark where so many of our heroes had worked their magic. In the distance, closer to the river, was the green spire of the Old Cathedral, a basilica for the devout since 1834. On our other side was Eads Bridge, the river's most cherished crossing.

We looked for the Mississippi, lost in the darkness and snow. Above us, the Arch shimmered in fiery streams of red, yellow, and green. A trio of young people standing nearby looked straight into the heavens at the fireworks. They saw us and came over to shake our hands and exchange New Year's greetings and hugs. We learned that they had just moved to Saint Louis and already had fallen deeply in love with the city.

We finally moved on and left the new Saint Louisans below the Arch, with the fireworks bursting above. We imagined what the scene must have looked like from just a few miles away on top of Monks Mound, cloaked in the quiet snow of yet another new year.

Meet me in St. Louis, Louis,
Meet me at the fair.
Don't tell me the lights are shining
Anyplace but there.

— Andrew B. Sterling and Kerry Mills
"Meet Me in St. Louis, Louis"

Ghost Towns

A term developed in the early twentieth century that refers to once thriving and active towns that have been deserted or nearly abandoned. Every state has its share, but the best known — usually former mining boomtowns — are in the American West. Some popular ghost towns are Bodie, California; Virginia City, Nevada; Jerome, Arizona; Shakespeare, New Mexico; and Terlingua, Texas. Some ghost towns make comebacks, but usually, once a town dies, it stays dead.

▪

There are enough celebrity ghost towns around for all the camera-toting tourists. Sometimes these places get so many visitors that folks finally move back to make a living off the visitors. That's what happened at Madrid, New Mexico, the old coal-mining community on the Turquoise Trail southwest of Santa Fe. The same is true of Oatman, the once bustling gold-mining town on a stretch of the original Route 66 high above the Arizona-California border. Swarms of people stop daily to look for ghosts in the

Oatman Hotel or to feed the semiwild burros that congregate downtown.

To see a ghost town in the making, go to yet another Route 66 relic — Glenrio, nestled right on the Texas-New Mexico line. That's where we usually pause going east or west on nearby Interstate 40, the superslab that did Glenrio in when it bypassed the town. Today there are more dogs than humans in Glenrio. It wasn't always that way. Once this town was as busy as a noontime greasy spoon.

Founded in 1903 in the grassy hollow of a small stream, the town has a name which combines the English word glen with the Spanish word for river. By 1916, a post office had opened for local merchants, railroaders, and cowboys from both sides of the state border. After Route 66 was constructed, the town prospered even more. By the time the highway was paved in the late 1930s, Glenrio supported several bustling cafes, bars, and tourist courts.

A constant stream of travelers, including dust bowl migrants, GIs going to war, salesmen, and ranchers, paused at this town straddling the state line. Depending on the direction of travel, for some it was the first stop in New Mexico, and for others it was the first in Texas. Glenrio was touted as the place where folks could have their picture made standing with one foot in the Lone Star State and the other in the Land of Enchantment.

DEAD END AHEAD

Life in Glenrio was sweeter than truck-stop pie. But then the government came along and changed all that. It built the fancy new highway and left the town high and dry. Pretty soon, some of the smaller businesses were forced to close. People started to pack up and move on. Weeds began to poke through the pavement. That's when the ghosts moved in. They are there today, just waiting for people to rediscover the town.

Behind the post office . . . is a row of seven desolate cabins. The doors are open and there are old naked mattresses and iron bed frames inside the tiny rooms. Nearby stands an elm tree as wide as the girth of four grown men, its bark covered with the dried skeletons of locusts that shed their skins and sang lonely August chants from the tree.

. . . Down the highway, a sign warns DEAD END AHEAD. Two roadrunners — speedy chaparrals — dash from the brush. The birds play tag on the pavement of the old road and then run off and vanish mysteriously in the New Mexican countryside.

— Michael Wallis
Route 66: The Mother Road

Greasy Grass

The Cheyenne, Sioux, and other tribal people's name for a stream that whites call the Little Bighorn. The ninety-mile-long river rises in the mountains of north-central Wyoming and flows north to the Bighorn River in south-central Montana.

▪

More painters and writers have converged on the Little Bighorn than on Gettysburg, which is puzzling. Erudite explanations compete with one another like professors at a cocktail party, yet none seems satisfactory.

— Evan S. Connell
Son of the Morning Star

No photographers were present in the southern part of Montana Territory on June 25, 1876, when more than two hundred men from the U.S. Army's Seventh Cavalry, led by Lieutenant Colonel George Armstrong Custer, advanced toward a Sioux encampment along the banks of a meandering stream named the River of Greasy Grass. No photographs exist of what transpired that hot afternoon as the two sides locked in deadly combat. The whites called it the Battle of the Little Bighorn or Custer's Last Stand, but to the Sioux the engagement became known as *Pe-hin* (Head-hair) *Hanska* (Long) *Ktepi* (Killed), or "the fight in which Long Hair was killed," after the thirty-six-year-old cavalry officer who usually wore his hair shoulder length.

In truth (something in short supply when it comes to stories of Custer), his reddish-gold locks had been cropped short before he and the troops departed Fort Abraham Lincoln, near Bismarck, Dakota Territory, on their fateful mission. The mission came to a sudden halt when that fabled "Custer's luck" — which had followed the flamboyant soldier throughout his checkered career — ran out. Later, around barracks games of chance, old soldiers mused that Custer was like the biblical Samson — his famous long hair had been the source of his strength.

Although the controversial Custer did not live to fulfill his own ambitions, his legend and heroic reputation grew, thanks to Buffalo Bill Cody's fictionalized reenactments of the "Last Stand" and the literary efforts of Elizabeth Bacon Custer, the slain soldier's widow. Libbie, as friends and family called her, wrote three best-selling books touting her husband's exploits and portraying him as a chivalrous symbol of courage. This diligent mythmaker amassed quite a sizable fortune before her death on New York's fashionable Park Avenue in 1933, fifty-seven years after her husband's demise on a windswept hillside.

One of the least understood yet most frequently depicted episodes in American history, the battle on the banks of the Greasy Grass has become the subject of literature, films, paintings, and drawings that have helped create a lasting — if mostly inaccurate — impression of what transpired. Thousands of renditions of the Custer battle have showed up in dime novels, magazines, comic books, bubblegum cards, and works of art.

Some of the first recorded pictures of the Greasy Grass battle appeared just a couple of weeks after the shocking news of "Custer's Last Stand" reached the cities along the East Coast. The cover of the *Illustrated Police News* weekly of July 13, 1876, showed Custer as the tragic hero with flowing hair and sword in hand. Clearly, the unnamed artist did not know about Custer's recent haircut or the fact that the troops had not taken their sabers along, but had left them at the fort. Since that first depiction, Custer has been portrayed in a variety of dramatic poses, wearing everything imaginable, from a full-dress uniform to his very best Hollywood buckskins complete with fringe to match his long locks. One of the more unusual versions of the battle scene is a painting by William R. Leigh which shows the Indian side of the conflict, with the mounted warriors firing their repeating rifles, and Custer and his men in the background, barely visible because of the great veil of yellowish dust.

Probably the best known of the many paintings is *Custer's Last Fight*, the original of which was painted on a tent fly by Cassily Adams. The artist completed his painting in 1886 after he had been provided with memories of the scene from various Indians who had witnessed the event, including the Crow scout Curly. The painting was hanging in a Saint Louis saloon when it came to the attention of Adolphus Busch, the beer magnate. In 1890, he acquired the painting and commissioned Otto Becker to copy it for use as a lithograph. The original Adams painting was presented to the Seventh Calvary in 1895. It was destroyed during a fire in the officers' club at Fort Bliss, in El Paso, on June 13, 1946, not quite seventy years after the battle took place. As many as a million lithographic copies of Becker's rendition of the Adams portrait were distributed by Anheuser-Busch. Many of them found their way to tavern walls where for years to come patrons toasted the memory of the mythical Custer. The famous barroom poster undoubtedly influenced such filmmakers as John Ford, who had hoped to be a fine artist and often framed his more memorable movie scenes as if they were oil paintings.

Despite the efforts of Edgar Samuel Paxson, John Mulvany, Frederic Remington, Charles Russell, and other notable artists, some of the most compelling depictions of the Greasy Grass battle were offered by Native Americans who were there. These works — such as a painting on muslin showing Sitting Bull during the Custer battle, as rendered by Iron Horse, a drawing on tanned buffalo hide by Lame Deer, and different views by Amos Bad Heart Buffalo, White Bird, and others — were collected along with verbal accounts of battlefield survivors.

Like their white counterparts, these artists sometimes made mistakes. Kicking Bear, a Sioux warrior, made sure the pictograph he created showed Custer accurately, without a saber and wearing buckskins, but he also presented the white leader with long hair — perhaps a bit of artistic license, because Custer's flowing locks were such an important part of his Sioux name. Bad Heart Buffalo, only a boy at the time of the battle, showed Custer confronting Crazy Horse and Sitting Bull, a scene that never took place.

In 1881, Red Horse drew the most comprehensive of the pictographs of that momentous day. The Sioux chief made a series of forty-one drawings with crayon and pencil on manila paper at the suggestion of a U.S. Army surgeon who realized that Red Horse had played a key role in the battle. These drawings, along with the detailed narrative that Red Horse conveyed in sign language, which was translated into English, yielded a memoir from the winners' side. Ironically, Custer is not shown in any of the Red Horse drawings. Perhaps that is the way it should be.

Grub

A word for food, a meal, or food supplies. Although not of western origin but supposedly a slang term dating to seventeenth-century England, its usage became common throughout the American West.

▪

If you are what you eat, then there are as many different species of westerners as there are stars in a clear prairie sky. All kinds of people — Native American, Spanish, German, Italian, Chinese, and so many others — have left their gastronomic tracks across the American West and have added to the annals of food lore.

Throughout the spicy history of the West, everything from roasted puppies and grasshoppers to buffalo steaks and coon-fat cake have been served for supper. Some folks have even dined on each other, as did the eighty-seven men, women, and children from the ill-fated Donner Party way back in 1846. The unlucky pioneers found themselves snowbound in the High Sierras of California, and had to resort to cannibalism to survive. Then there was

Alferd Packer, the prospector who became known as the "Colorado Cannibal." The twenty-one men he was leading through the backcountry became snowbound, and Alferd was left with no choice but to dine on some of his companions rather than starve. At his subsequent trial, the judge was supposed to have cracked that there were no more Democrats left in San Juan County because Packer had eaten them all — or so the story goes.

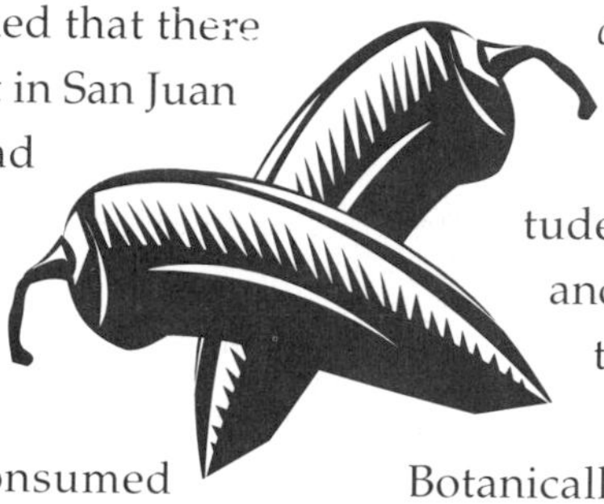

Despite the interesting variety of dishes that has been concocted and consumed throughout the West, we still maintain a fondness for down-home vittles such as the blue-plate specials — home-cooked food made with care and sweat — served along Route 66 and at authentic diners and greasy spoons. We also like standard cowpoke chow — or at least the idea of it. Our mouths water over the thought of hot meals baked in Dutch ovens and dished out from the back of a chuck wagon. Whenever we see one of those old-time western movies with "Saturday's heroes" sitting around the campfire eating a plate of beans and bacon and washing it down with tin mugs of stout coffee, we get as hungry as bears.

But the single food staple that makes us howl at the moon is the piquant, savory, peerless — and misunderstood — chile. We are not alone. The mere mention of the word — whether *chile* for the peppers or *chili* for the meat dish made from them — can bring tears of anguish or bliss to multitudes of people. The chile, an ancient symbol, glorious spice, tangy condiment, is the soul food of the gods.

Botanically a fruit but commercially a vegetable, the chile was not developed by Spaniards, but was one of the earliest plants cultivated by the ancient Indians of the Americas. Some chile seeds found in Mexican excavations date from 7,000 B.C. Known as "Chilli" to the Aztecs, the pods of this versatile plant were in abundant use before Columbus splashed ashore. He discovered Indians cultivating ancestors of today's chile, and he mistakenly called the plant "pepper" because of its pungency.

Deeply rooted in the history of the Aztecs, this plant with its hundreds of varieties has spread throughout Latin America, jumped the border, and consumed the Rocky Mountain West. The love of chile went on to cross the continent at a prairie-fire clip. Like cowboy boots, blue jeans, and tequila, chile became respectable.

Still, the truth, the whole truth about chile can be found in the growing fields and kitchens of New Mexico. It is there that chile is most cherished. New Mexicans eat more chile per capita than anyone else. They grow it in backyard gardens and munch raw chiles like candy. Chile is the fiery essence of New Mexico. Some aficionados would just as soon give the plant deity status.

Chile pilgrims, hungry for action, should make the trek to New Mexico in the autumn. That is the perfect season — aspens are at their glory, piñon smoke hangs in the air, and ripe chiles are brought in from the fields.

Our periodic chile odysseys usually begin in Santa Fe, the haunt of the chic and the vacuous but also home for a few genuine artists, and a formidable base of operations for true chile connoisseurs. For many years, we launched most of our New Mexican adventures, including chile quests, at an adobe studio on Canyon Road. There, surrounded by smart shops and tourist traps, dwelled Bill Tate, a writer, painter, superb storyteller, and pure songdog. Tate is long gone from this earth, but his legacy in the form of tall tales and stories lingers like the echoes of a coyote's howl.

Tate kept the wolf from his door and gasoline in his dusty old Lincoln Continental by peddling watercolors and loads of booklets he published which chronicled his life and much of the history of New Mexico. He received visitors to his studio, including those curious about chile, at a cluttered desk surrounded by easels, half-finished paintings, books, bundles of letters, and religious statuary. Every nook and cranny was filled with treasures — potsherds, six-shooters, branding irons, stray coffee mugs, and a skull sporting wire-rimmed eyeglasses. Spiders worked in the windows, and an unknown creature that lived with the eccentric artist as long as we knew him could be heard rummaging inside the cupboards. A radio droned from beneath a mound of Indian blankets and decades-old newspapers. The smell of cooked chiles was almost always present, permeating the atmosphere.

We had dubbed Tate "Mr. New Mexico." Some of his old friends still called him "Judge" in honor of his brief tenure as a justice of the peace in the mountain village of Truchas. A few of us also knew Tate was a high priest of chile — self-proclaimed, of course. To hear him talk, he had eaten as much chile as any Anglo in the Southwest. Maybe he had.

"If you want to start the day off right, then eat plenty of chile — the fresher the better," Tate would tell us. He kept a tank of oxygen next to his bed and his hacking cough never improved, but there was always a pan of chili simmering on his big blue iron stove and a *ristra*, or string, of red chiles hanging on the wall like a vegetable rosary. "Got to have that chile close to me," Tate would say. "The older I get, the more I appreciate it."

Tate loved to speak of a Hispanic lady he knew who made green-chile mulch every autumn. "This woman was big and fat," Tate told us. "She must have weighed well over three hundred pounds. She'd have a big batch of cooked chili, and she would dig her hands right into the pot and be scrunching and squeezing that stuff. Every once in a while she'd put a fistful of the chili in her mouth. Then she'd let out a bloodcurdling scream and run out the front door and into the road, jumping up and down, fanning her open mouth, and screaming, 'Oh, my God, that's so hot! That's so hot!' Finally, she'd cool down a little bit and she'd be sweating all over and shaking and she'd come back inside with a look of ecstasy in her eyes and say, 'Oh, that is such good chili; it is so very fine.' And then she'd start all over again."

Unless brave gourmets sample a "bowl of blessedness," as Will Rogers called properly cooked chili, they will have no inkling of what Tate and the fat lady loved to ladle generously on nearly everything they consumed — from fried eggs to sirloin steak.

Despite all the goodness chile brings, the misconceptions still abound. Adlai Stevenson, a very wise man, once said, "A great deal of what North Americans think they know about Central and South America isn't so." He could have been talking about the Hispanic Southwest and the misconceptions about chile. Except for tequila, the snappy Mexican beverage, no other Latin American commodity has been as maligned as the noble chile.

Perhaps the main misconception about the chile is its red-hot reputation. Some chiles are fiery hot to the taste and touch, but several varieties are quite mild, even sweet. Chile's hotness comes from capsaicin, a devilish chemical concentrated in the interior veins, or ribs, near the seed heart. When a chile pod is sliced open and the veins have a yellowish-orange tone, count on the chile being potent.

There are remedies if a person should have the unfortunate luck of getting even a hint of lethal chile juice on the tongue or, God forbid, in the eye. Old-timers such as Tate, with plenty of chile-burn scar tissue to attest to their wisdom, often told us, "A bit of sugar on your tongue takes the chile sting from the eye." Tate also swore by a poultice of dry tortilla applied directly to the trouble spot after a thorough cold-water rinse.

In some of the more remote mountain villages of New Mexico, sages still swear that lightly brushing human hair over the eyes also brings quick relief from hot chile. In the case of fire in the throat and mouth, milk and beer can help, and so can chewing bread or sopaipillas. Some restaurants along the border, including a few of our old favorites in El Paso and Juárez, are known to keep bunches of ripe bananas in strategic locations for emergencies involving high-octane chile overdoses.

Common sense helps. If possible, avoid problems by placing a pinch of salt on the tongue tip to raise a protective layer of saliva before eating a hot chile. It is wise to remember that most any chile can be cooled before eating by simply removing the seeds where the offending hotness collects. When preparing chiles for sauces and relishes, a long soak in hot milk or water helps to tame the fire. But the faint at heart should remember that no one has ever perished from chile burnout — at least, not yet.

Maybe it was Bill Tate — our high priest of chile — who summed it up best with this benediction: "Chile is New Mexico's 'caviar,' and just as precious. It should be exported all over the world as one of the great luxury foods. There is nothing to equal our chile."

Amen.

Harvey Girls

Popular name for the women who worked, from the 1880s to the 1950s, in the restaurants established by Fred Harvey, the consummate host who later was known as the "civilizer of the West." Harvey Houses were found mostly along the Atchison, Topeka & Santa Fe Railway and at key tourist destinations throughout the western half of the United States.

▪

Born in London in 1835, Fred Harvey traveled to the United States as a young man. We have him to thank for bringing a special touch of class to the rambunctious western half of the country when it was sorely needed. Diners at a Harvey House had to be attired suitably; even cowboys were required to wear proper coats.

After working his way west from New York, Harvey ultimately opened a series of restaurants that stretched along three thousand miles of railroad lines crossing the West. His genteel taste was reflected not only in the architecture of his establishments but also in the variety and quality of menus and his rules of social etiquette. No swearing was permitted in a Harvey House.

But perhaps one of the most profound influences that Fred Harvey had on the social evolution of the West was his recruitment of young ladies "of good character, attractive, and intelligent" to become waitresses in his eating houses. Promising not to marry for at least a year, teachers, nurses, and romantics in search of adventure answered the call.

▪

As children, we had the pleasure of dining in some of the Harvey Houses scattered from Chicago to San Francisco. What made these occasions memorable were the remarkable women who wore the distinctive Harvey Girl uniforms. Once we were seated, they made us feel like part of their dining-room family. They seemed to embrace us like familiar aunts as they delivered fresh shrimp cocktails, club steaks, whipped potatoes, green garden peas, and peach sundaes.

One of these "women who opened the West" has become a cherished friend. Her name is Lillian Redman. Her combination of spunk and grace has always seemed to epitomize the spirit of the Harvey Girls, who prided themselves on serving up quality food and plenty of genuine hospitality. Lillian came to New Mexico from Texas with her homesteader parents in a covered wagon. She invested many years of her life as a waitress and a cook at Harvey Houses throughout the Southwest before settling in Tucumcari to preside as hostess at the legendary Blue Swallow Motel.

From time to time, we visit Lillian. During our western treks, we also pay our respects to some of the great Harvey Houses — those that are boarded up and others still in operation. Some of these hotels are as familiar to us as the homes in which we grew up. We have walked the cool halls of El Garces at blistering Needles and waved good-bye to pals boarding a Santa Fe train at La Posada, the replica of a Spanish rancho in Winslow. We watched the senseless demolition of the graceful Alvarado Hotel in the heart of Albuquerque, and have hosted luncheons in the main dining room of El Tovar, perched on the south rim of the Grand Canyon.

The Harvey House we hold most dear is La Fonda, "the Inn at the End of the Santa

Fe Trail." When we were learning to flex our creative wings, both of us worked at La Fonda, the most historic and distinctive hotel in Santa Fe. This bastion of hospitality and cheer not only provided us with income but also many memorable experiences. We forged friendships with colorful and eccentric poets, artists, and raconteurs who taught us some of their best songdog lyrics and tricks. We watched movie stars and celebrities stroll through the lobby. We met Thorton Wilder in the cozy cantina. And we came to accept the premise that if the time-worn plaza is the heart of Santa Fe, then surely La Fonda is the essence of the ancient city's exuberant soul. It is Santa Fe's living room.

Besides working as an executive secretary and a dining-room waiter at La Fonda during those same lean early days, we also were employed by a great-grandson of the esteemed Fred Harvey. We soon learned that this descendant of the illustrious host and purveyor to the West did not hold a candle to his famous ancestor when it came to dispensing hospitality. Still, we persevered and managed to learn some valuable lessons from our brief tenure with him.

Our young boss had once been part of the Harvey family business but was anxious to make his own mark. One of his many endeavors was a ski resort lodge, complete with guest rooms, bar, and restaurant. Our task was to manage the lodge, check in guests and clean their rooms, prepare and provide all meals, and tend the very busy bar. Several of our fellow creative coconspirators, the Spinners, worked with us.

As the snow flew and the ski season progressed, it became all too clear that our Mr. Harvey was far too busy expanding his restaurant operations in the lowlands to be concerned with the ski lodge far away on the lofty slopes. Frequently we were left high and dry and our pleas for help went unanswered when our frazzled employer failed to send fresh food and other provisions to us. We soon learned how to improvise.

One morning, with every room in the lodge booked, we faced a capacity crowd of half-starved Texans and Okies in the dining room, all primed and ready to tangle with steak and eggs before hitting the slopes to learn — as they did year after year — how to snowplow. To our dismay, the food order we had placed had not been trucked to our kitchen during the night. The cupboard was bare. There were no eggs, no breakfast meats, and not a single drop of milk.

As our anxious guests' stomachs began to rumble, we had a brainstorm. We went to the bar and mixed a reservoir of frothy tequila sunrises. "These are on the house!" we shouted as we delivered glasses of semifresh o.j. to the kids and mugs brimming with liquid courage to the adults.

Back in the kitchen, we broke into our cache of succulent rainbow trout and fried every one of them to crispy perfection. Garnished with sliced tomatoes and sprigs of piñon pine, the platters of trout were carried, along with baskets of steaming tortillas, to the dining room where, by then, the potent tequila sunrises had fully risen. No one left hungry or unhappy, and most of the guests declared it was the best breakfast they had ever had — bar none.

That afternoon, a truck overflowing with supplies rumbled up to the lodge. We breathed sighs of relief. But as the sun set in the west and our thirsty skiers, refreshed by hot showers, padded to the bar for their evening libation by the roaring fire, we found we were beset by yet another seemingly insurmountable problem. The cranky old ice machine we had continually asked our employer to replace had given up the ghost. We were facing a bar packed with customers, and we were completely out of ice.

Just as we were about to propose that they give up their usual highballs for hot toddies, inspiration struck once more. In a heartbeat, we were outside in the frigid darkness filling laundry baskets and buckets with the gleaming icicles that hung like stalactites from the eaves and gutters. Back at the crowded bar, we chilled every bourbon and scotch by thrusting a pair of icicles into each glass.

"These are New Mexico swizzle sticks," we declared. "Cheers!"

In the wee hours, after every guest was tucked away for the night and all that remained of the fire were a few glowing embers, we snacked on cold leftover trout and toasted our resourcefulness with glasses of milk chilled with stalks of ice. Through it all, we had managed to remain the consummate hosts.

Old Fred Harvey would have been mighty proud.

Buddy Holly

1936-1959. Born Charles Hardin Buddy Holley (he later dropped the *e*) in Lubbock, Texas, this popular musician became a true rock and roll martyr when he died at age twenty-two in a plane crash with two other famous singers—seventeen-year-old Richie Valens and J.P. "Big Bopper" Richardson, twenty-eight. Also killed was Roger Peterson, the twenty-one-year-old pilot.

▪

On February 3, 1959, when that small plane en route to Fargo, North Dakota, carrying Holly, Valens, and Richardson crashed in a snow-covered cornfield near Clear Lake, Iowa, the shock waves reached millions of teenage fans. We were among those left stunned.

It was a triple whammy. Those of us in America's heartland were partial to the Big Bopper and sang his "Chantilly Lace" every chance we got. Out in the Texas borderland, we were drawn to the rhythmic beat of "La Bamba," the Mexican folk song Valens had resurrected to capture the hearts of Hispanic and Anglo teens. All of us shared a passion for the music of Buddy Holly, the bespectacled West Texas warbler. He combined the best of Elvis and Little Richard and allowed us to feel cool as we listened to music as sweet as a cherry Coke laced with bourbon, as exciting as a backseat romp in a steamed-up Chevy.

Years later, after the deaths of Jimi Hendricks, Janis Joplin, and Jim Morrison, we all knew who Don McLean was memorializing in "American Pie," his haunting 1971 hit song about "the day the music died." It was a tribute to Buddy Holly, who didn't overdose on drugs or success but crashed and burned in a Bonanza Beechcraft with Valens and the Big Bopper, like a trio of rookie songbirds flying too close to the ground.

During his fleeting lifetime, Holly churned out forty-five songs. All of them were hits, but most fans remember "It's So Easy," "Oh Boy," "It Doesn't Matter Any More," "Everyday," and his classic "Peggy Sue." We danced to all of them, but the one Holly song we'll always cherish is "That'll Be the Day." Although there are loads of good Holly yarns, as related in books, films, and articles, the most telling is the simple story of how "That'll Be the Day" became his first hit tune.

It all started in Buddy's hometown of Lubbock in the late spring of 1956. He and two of his pals went to the State Theater on Texas Avenue to catch the latest John Ford flick — *The Searchers.* The film starred none other than John Wayne in the role of Ethan Edwards, an ex-Confederate who returns to the Texas frontier in 1868 to find that his brother, sister-in-law, and their son have been killed by Comanches. Even worse, especially for a macho white man, his dead brother's two daughters were carried off by the "heathen savages." Ethan Edwards, as played by the Duke, gets right on the girls' trail. The oldest one is found dead, but the Indian-hating Edwards persists for several more years until he finally finds his younger niece, portrayed by a doe-eyed Natalie Wood.

Throughout the 119-minute movie, the stalwart Edwards frequently grumbles a catch phrase, "That'll be the day," as he continues to search for the lost girl. Those words apparently stuck in Holly's fertile mind. Days later when he was tinkering with a new tune, Buddy heard one of his friends use that same phrase in conversation. Holly thought his friend was suggesting it as the title for their song. He liked the sound of it. Later that summer, Buddy went to Nashville and recorded his first version of the now legendary "That'll Be the Day." The Decca producers convinced Holly to sing it like a slow country-western song, and he did. The result was disastrous. Hardly anyone liked it, and the tune festered on the shelf.

But seven months later, Holly and his band drove over to the Clovis, New Mexico, studio of Norman Petty and recorded another version of "That'll Be the Day." This time Buddy did it his way — pure rockabilly, with energy and pep. When finally released in May of 1957, it gradually began to climb the charts. Thanks at first to fans back east, the song became a Buddy Holly classic. It still is.

Home on the Range

Traditional cowboy song with melancholy tune that apparently evolved during the 1880s. Several versions and titles exist, including "An Arizona Home" and "Colorado Home," with claims of authorship in dispute. Some music historians credit the music and words to C.O. Swartz, but others believe the lyrics were written by a Kansas homesteader. Regardless of origin, the song remains a true classic of the West and is known widely as the "cowboy's national anthem." Perfect for singing on a winter night inside the home of your choice before a roaring fire.

■

When deciding on our favorite home on the range, all kinds of choices dance through our minds — from Navajo hogans and the snug tepee and buffalo-skin lodges of the Plains Indians to the dugouts or soddies that sodbusters made from prairie turf to the ubiquitous log cabin, usually constructed of lodgepole pines chinked with mud, stone, and grass. All of them have their pluses, but there is one kind of house we find more comfortable than all the rest — adobe.

Once you live in an adobe, you will be spoiled. There has never been a more comfortable dwelling than a house of plastered bricks fashioned from handfuls of *la Santa Madre Tierra,* "the Holy Mother Earth." The most forgiving of building materials because you can cover a multitude of architectural sins in a house made of mud, adobe, with its thick walls, is cool in summer and warm in winter.

Used thousands of years ago by early Egyptians and Babylonians, adobe, named from a Spanish word of Arabic origin, consists of sun-dried bricks made of sandy clay, straw, and water. Adobe is also the specially prepared mud from which the bricks are made, as well as the architecture constructed of the material. Adobe provided Pueblo Indians and early Spanish settlers throughout the arid

Southwest with shelter, fortresses, and places of worship.

The earthen bricks have been used in Santa Fe to build the oldest house still standing in the United States, at Santa Fe, the ancient Taos Pueblo, and many other edifices ranging from ultrachic hideaways to modest dwellings tucked away in remote mountain hamlets.

No matter if it's a palace or a hut, if it has stood a century or if the plaster is still wet, an adobe seems more a part of the past than of the present.

The bricks serve as a form of memory. They furnish evidence of the past. When the plaster falls off old buildings, the exposed adobes may reveal traces of deer which had come in late spring to nibble the straw in the newly made bricks, leaving hoofprints frozen in time. The etched palms of generations long gone and bits of animal bone and rock give texture to the thick walls.

— Michael Wallis (text) and Craig Varjabedian (photography)
En Divina Luz: The Penitente Moradas of New Mexico

Indian Territory

A region assigned to various Indian tribes for their own use in what became the state of Oklahoma in 1907. Surrounded by Missouri, Arkansas, Texas, and Kansas, this land was populated largely by tribes organized into "Nations," supposedly protected by treaties with the United States.

■

Oklahoma history did not commence with the celebrated land runs of 1889 and 1893. The hunk of real estate made up of Oklahoma and Indian Territories, along with a narrow panhandle called "No Man's Land," enjoyed a rich history prior to becoming the forty-sixth state of the Union. Long before the swarms of white settlers raced across the borders to grab tracts of property, the "Twin Territories" were home to all sorts of people.

There is a rather simple story that describes Oklahoma's birth as a state. It tells of a Cherokee woman and her husband, a white man who was anxious to take part in the festivities of November 16, 1907, when

President Theodore Roosevelt issued the statehood proclamation.

Instead of going with her husband to the big celebration, the Cherokee woman stayed home. When her husband returned, he proudly told his wife that at long last they no longer lived in the Cherokee Nation, but were citizens of the state of Oklahoma. She did not share his joy. Instead, the woman began to cry. She went to bed and cried all night long. Her heart was broken. She could not bear to think that her Cherokee Nation and her people's land had been transformed into another part of the white man's domain.

▪

Although it has been some time since we adopted Oklahoma as our home, we have never taken the place for granted. We are still drawn to the distinctive spirit at the heart of this state that takes its name from the old Choctaw phrase meaning "red people."

Two extraordinary women who have become our friends best represent for us the essence of two of the main cultures — Anglo and Native American — that collided long before Oklahoma became a state, but later merged in America's heartland. Both of these Oklahomans maintain strong ties to the past — an important reservoir of strength and knowledge for them to draw from as they impact the present and consider the future.

▪

We became acquainted with Wilma Mankiller, the first woman to lead a major Native American tribe, just before she became principal chief of the Cherokee Nation. Our first meeting was at her home on 160 acres of ancestral property in the rolling hills of eastern Oklahoma. We shared stories and ideas. She was easy to be with. From the beginning, we felt as though we had known her forever.

Wilma's quiet strength, dignity, and resolve, along with an abiding sense of her heritage, have helped shape this woman who has looked death directly in the eye on several occasions and emerged as the victor. Without a trace of pretense but with commitment, curiosity, and wonder, Wilma and her husband, Charlie Soap, move comfortably with power brokers and world leaders as easily as they do among their neighbors and friends in rural Oklahoma. They are true children of the 1960s, and they epitomize the very best of the rich Indian Territory legacy that can still be found on the prairies, in the cities and small towns, and throughout the woodlands of Oklahoma.

One of the many reasons we are attracted to Wilma is her deep love of the land, particularly the place that has come to be known as Oklahoma.

We have walked with Wilma at Mankiller Flats, surrounded by 160 acres of ancestral property allotted to her paternal grandfather, John Mankiller, when Oklahoma became a state. We have sat with her on her front porch and listened to cardinals and mockingbirds sing from the redbud trees. We have visited with people from all over the world inside Wilma's snug house, warmed by a stove fed by firewood cut from the nearby forest.

"If I am to be remembered," Wilma told us, "I want it to be because I am fortunate enough to have become my tribe's first female chief. But I also want to be remembered for emphasizing the fact that we have indigenous solutions to our problems. Cherokee values, especially those of helping one another and of our interconnections with the land, can be used to address contemporary issues."

No matter where we may go, we will always remember Wilma's wise words.

▪

Lydia Lloyd Wyckoff whirled into our lives like a renegade cyclone, but from the start we knew her power was not destructive. Armed with a Ph.D. in anthropology and an unquenchable thirst for knowledge, Lydia returned to her Oklahoma roots after years of sharpening her mind and nurturing her soul in London, Connecticut, and Miami, from the far reaches of Africa to the ageless pueblos at Zuñi and Hopi and the canyon lands of the Navajo.

Her father, of good Welsh stock, came from Pennsylvania to teach economics in

Oklahoma when the state was still in its early twenties. He met a schoolteacher in an oil-patch town in the Osage, and they married. Eventually, they moved to England, where they raised a son named Roger and a daughter — our friend Lydia.

During the German blitz of London in World War II, Roger and Lydia were sent to live with their mother's family in Oklahoma. In the Osage country, there were no air-raid sirens and splintered churches. There were cow ponies to ride and the sound of oil-field pump jacks keeping time on the prairie. While they attended a country school made of native stone and learned to love the blackjack oaks and unending sea of bluestem grass, Lydia and her brother became acquainted with their past.

They heard stories of ancestors who had driven ox teams across the West, and of a cowboy grandfather who had traded his life as a rider on the Chisholm Trail to become a country doctor so he could gain "respectability" and marry the young woman of his dreams. There were more stories of their grandfather having made the "run" and staking his claim in 1893 when the Cherokee Outlet was opened, of a kinsman who had served as Indian agent at Pawhuska and later was governor of Oklahoma Territory, and of pioneer relatives who had become artists, political and civic leaders, and ranchers.

When we visit Lydia and stay in the old home with thick stone walls that she has restored, we sometimes sleep in a bed that once belonged to the last territorial governor. The rooms of the big house are filled with art, books, and treasures — some from Great Britain, some from New England, and some from the other lands and places that Lydia has called home. A zebra skin is stretched across the living-room floor, the horns of a longhorn steer hang over the main fireplace, a framed photograph of Teddy Roosevelt taken during a Rough Rider recruiting trip graces a library table. The walls and shelves hold art of the Osages and other tribal peoples.

And on the long, gleaming dining table is a bronze statue of a pair of riders, one in fancy dress astride an English saddle on a prancing steed, and the other, a cowboy on his reliable quarter horse, coming over to help the first rider. The figures represent the two parts of our friend's life.

That melding is apparent on those special evenings, after a dinner of venison or roasted quail, when every chair around the table is filled with Osage and city friends, ranchers and family. The conversations dart from literature, history, and politics to Osage County gossip, beef prices, and the threat of storms.

Outside, beyond the fences and the thickets of sumac and sassafras — whether there is a full moon or not — we can count on a family of coyotes to break into song, just as they have been doing since long, long ago when there was no state of Oklahoma, no Indian Territory, and nobody knew the difference.

Jackalope

A mythical creature — with a jackrabbit body, deer antlers, and the speed of an antelope — whose range includes much of the western United States.

▪

Throughout the history of the American West, there have been all sorts of folk yarns, myths, and tall tales of men and beasts. Most of these spellbinders are best told around a campfire or in a well-stocked bar.

We never grow weary of hearing the exploits of Pecos Bill — the legendary Texas character who was brought up by a coyote, educated by a grizzly, and rode Widow Maker, an ornery horse raised on a diet of barbed wire and nitroglycerin.

Reports of UFOs in the skies over New Mexico, unexplained ghost lights in western Texas and eastern Oklahoma, and a slew of unsolved mysteries, hauntings, and ghost stories from Houston to Seattle help keep our minds open. And we won't forget the accounts of the elusive creature known as Sasquatch (a.k.a. Bigfoot) we heard in the Pacific Northwest from drunk and sober loggers, Native American wisdom keepers, and even professors of anthropology.

Still, nothing and no one tickles our imagination and fancy like the jackalope. Although some cynics insist that this whimsical animal is strictly the creation of an imaginative taxidermist with a few spare critter parts, some mind-altering whiskey or peyote, and a great deal of time on his hands, we choose to believe otherwise.

Fact is, we've seen several stunning examples of jackalopes at some of our favorite hangouts scattered throughout the West. There's a jackalope big enough to saddle and ride at Wall Drug in South Dakota. In northern Arizona, a handsome mounted jackalope head adorns the wall at the Jack Rabbit Trading Post, known far and wide for its sweet cherry cider and its familiar signs displaying a crouched rabbit silhouette.

Naturally, there are several tales about how these outrageous creatures came to be. The more conventional version has it that the very first jackalope was born in Douglas, Wyoming, in 1934 when a couple of taxidermists took it upon themselves to attach the antlers of a small dead deer to the skull of a freshly road-killed jackrabbit. After gluing their creation to a slab of wood, they tacked it above the bar at a local saloon, where — no doubt after only a brief glance at the jackalope — many an established drunk swore to take the pledge.

Yet another theory, and the one we adhere to, claims that jackalopes always have been around the West — from the Mexican to the Canadian borders — and the first white person to see one was a trapper named George McLean, in 1829. It is said that when McLean later made the mistake of talking about the small beast, he was branded immediately as a bold-faced liar.

Although most of them won't dare admit it for fear of suffering the same fate as McLean, more than one cowboy singing to a herd of cattle at night has been surprised to hear a melancholy melody bounce back from the hills and mesas. Old-timers believe the phantom echo is some lonely jackalope wailing its heart out. They say the jackalope songs are heard mostly on pitch-black nights just before a thunderstorm. Campfire stories that jackalopes sometimes get together and sing in chorus are usually discounted by those who know the creatures best.

Justins

A once common moniker for western-style boots. The name originated from Herman Joseph "Daddy Joe" Justin, a cobbler in Spanish Fort, Texas, who started to make boots in 1879 for cowboys and drovers of longhorn cattle up the Chisholm Trail. By 1890, Justin had moved his boot-making operation to Nocona, seventeen miles south of Spanish Fort. To this day, most worthwhile boot makers credit Justin with having made the first genuine pair of cowboy boots.

▪

It was in Texas that we heard about a rancher who bought a pair of new boots that turned out to be too tight. The embarrassed boot maker insisted that he would stretch them.

"Not on your life," said the rancher. "These boots are going to stay too tight. When I get out of bed, I have to go round up some cattle that have busted out during the night, and mend the fences they've torn down. Every waking moment, I watch my ranch blow away in the dust and listen to news about the high cost of feed and the low price of beef. All the while, my wife is nagging me to sell out and move to town.

"When I get ready for bed and pull off those tight ol' boots — well, pard, that's the only real pleasure I get all day."

Tight boots aside, one thing is certain. No matter if they are ostrich skin or cowhide, pointy-toed with slung heels and manure caked on the sole or gleaming go-to-town boots with a fancy inlaid design on the sides, the absolute best — the rootin'est, tootin'est cowboy boots in the world — come from Texas.

Even though fine boot cobblers operate in Oklahoma, Arizona, and Kansas, we know that the Michelangelos of cowboy boot makers hail from the Lone Star State. The cowboy boot's revered place in the heritage of Texas comes largely from the famous boot-making families who settled there. The Lamas, Justins, Luccheses, and others left their distinctive marks.

When Suzanne and her brothers were growing up in El Paso, their folks took them on yearly pilgrimages to get new boots for the rodeo and, most of the time, Tony Lama himself waited on them.

Beside the big boot manufacturers, there were the individual boot makers — old masters who turned out handmade boots that anyone would be proud to pull on. Through the years, I was lucky to meet some of them.

In Austin, there was Charlie Dunn, a third-generation boot maker who made his first pair of cowboy boots in 1909, when he was eleven. When a cobbler can simply touch hides and select the best ones for first-rate cowboy boots, folks like to say the boot maker has "educated fingers." If that is true, then Charlie Dunn's fingers had a Ph.D. He never missed.

"People come to me and want to know about boot making. They want to know about coming into this trade," Charlie told me a few years before he died in 1993, at age ninety-five. "They come to me and ask how long it would take them to learn the boot business. I just look them straight in the eye and ask: 'How long do you expect to live?' You have to work at boot making all your life to get it right. If you can't give it your all, then don't even start."

There were others. Before he passed away in 1980, I spent time with Sam Lucchese, a soft-spoken genius with boot leather, who shod LBJ, John Wayne, General George Patton, Gene Autry, and Gary Cooper, to name but a few. Recognized as the foremost designer of cowboy boots in the world, Sam was a member of the famed Sicilian family that founded its San Antonio boot company in 1883 in the shadow of the Alamo. Teddy Roosevelt and his Rough Riders wore Luccheses up San Juan Hill. Like his father and grandfather before him, Sam studied the human foot, which he once told me is "the most magnificent piece of engineering in all of nature." Even though Sam is gone and the family no longer makes boots, Texans still say that after God created human feet, he made the Lucchese family to look after them.

I became acquainted with still other great boot makers, including Buck Steiner, Tony Lama Jr., Henry Leopold, Ray Jones, and T.O. Stanley.

Then I met the queen herself — Enid Justin.

I first shook her hand exactly 101 years after her legendary father — H.J. "Daddy Joe" Justin — had invented cowboy boots. I was told that Miss Enid, as most folks called her, could be found just below the Red River border in Nocona, a north-central Texas town named for the fiery Comanche Chief Peta Nocona (Pe-ta Nokoni). It was the place where "Daddy Joe" eventually moved his cowboy-boot operation.

They were dead right. I drove straight to tiny Nocona, and there she was — the grande dame of cowboy boots, sitting behind the desk in her tidy office at the Nocona Boot Company headquarters. Well into her eighties at the time, Miss Enid had every silver hair in place. A slight trace of Shalimar perfume hung in the air. Although a nephew and some others helped her to manage the firm, there was little doubt that the fiery Miss Enid was still very much in command of the company. She had founded it in 1925 after her brothers decided to move the family's Justin Boot Company to the bigger city of Fort Worth.

"I didn't want to move," she told me. "I just couldn't do that. I felt Daddy Joe would have stayed right here. Besides, being here without my brothers didn't worry me. I cut my teeth on leather."

Enid Justin was twelve years old when she started to stitch boots at her father's side. She had been suspended from school for dancing at her brother's birthday party. "We had a narrow-minded school board," she explained. "I decided not to go back to school. I went to work. I was my daddy's gal, and whatever I wanted I got from him."

Daddy Joe Justin had the bullheadedness of his Prussian ancestors. He knew from the start what he was cut out to do. He did not want to be a tailor like his father or a cigar maker like his brother. He wanted to make boots. When he was twenty, he left his home in Lafayette, Indiana, and went to Texas to work as a cobbler.

Justin ended up in Spanish Fort, a settlement established by the Spanish three centuries before. The Spaniards were long gone and the fort had become part of the Texas dust. The town of twenty buildings and two hundred citizens was a jumping-off point for outlaws who had only to splash across the Red River into Indian Territory to escape snooping law officers.

When he arrived in town in 1879, young Justin had a hammer, an awl, and two "shinplasters" — paper currency worth a quarter. The local barber took pity on Justin and backed him with a loan of thirty-five dollars. Justin set up shop in a small wooden building that also served as his residence. The sign he hung over the front door said : "H.J. Justin, Bootmaker." Whether the first pair of boots he made went to some footsore cowboy right off the nearby Chisholm Trail or to the barber will never be known. What is known is that Daddy Joe Justin started to make cowboy boots that fit like a glove.

Word spread far and fast about Justin and his talent for making quality boots. He hired helpers and, with the coming of the railroad, moved to Nocona, where he made boots for a variety of customers. Charles Russell wore Justins. So did Pancho Villa and Will Rogers. Heads of state, bandits, Texas Rangers, and silent screen cowpokes kept Justin boots in the public eye. A favorite family yarn spoke of three cattle thieves strung up from a tree limb near Wichita Falls. All three died with their boots on — and all of them were wearing Justins.

In 1908, the name of the firm was changed to H.J. Justin & Sons. By 1911, the average price of a pair of Justins was a hefty eleven dollars. Five years later, with his health failing, Daddy Joe turned over the business to his children. He died in 1918, leaving a legacy that would carry his name around the world.

By remaining in Nocona, at first, it seemed Enid might fail, as her brothers had warned. "Most cowboys shied away from buying boots from a woman," she told me, "but plain hard work kept us going." Miss Enid took in boarders, sold coal, and made seventy-five-cent hot lunches to keep the wolf from the door. She became her first salesperson, bumping up and down dusty West Texas cattle trails in a Model T Ford. Her diligence paid off.

When I met her, Miss Enid still adhered to a routine of hard work. She was up before dawn every day, including the Sabbath, at her pink stucco house topped by a cowboy-boot weathervane. Parked outside was her trusty pink Cadillac with "EJ BOOT" custom license plates.

That evening, after we had had a good visit and I had toured the boot plant, I went with Miss Enid to the cemetery on the edge of town, where an oil pump kept time among the tombstones and mockingbirds nested in the cedars. At the Justin plot, she put fresh flowers on her daughter's grave and glanced at a grave site reserved for her, with the name and birthdate already chiseled in the granite. Nearby, she paused at the graves of her parents, H.J. Justin and his wife, Annie. "I honor 'Daddy Joe' every day of my life," smiled the daughter of the man who made the first cowboy boots. We stood there for a long time, not saying anything else, but just listening to a gentle prairie wind.

Miss Enid joined her folks in 1990. She will always be at "Daddy Joe's" side.

Kachina

Pronounced kuh-CHEE-nuh. In Hopi, the word *kachi* means spirit or life, and *Na* means father. *Kachina* has three meanings: a spirit; a ceremonial impersonator; and a *tihü*, a carved replica doll. Of all the southwestern Pueblo people, the Hopi and Zuñi are associated most closely with the kachina.

▪

Ogres with goggled eyes...a winged mother with turquoise face edged in black feathers...Ahöla, whose mask is a sifter basket adorned by the symbol for stars ... thin red ears framing black and yellow faces. They wear collars of evergreen, fur, or shells, and they carry army swords, golden rattles, bows and arrows, sleigh bells, or baskets of beans. All different and yet the same, these are the Kachinam — messengers of the gods.

Miniature carved versions can be found lining the shelves of countless galleries and shops throughout the Southwest. Tourists flock to the Grand Canyon, Flagstaff, Santa Fe, Taos, and other popular haunts to buy kachina dolls and Native American art and crafts. Without knowing what these figures represent, dowagers dripping in turquoise and silver jewelry and newlyweds from back east grab up kachinas carved from cottonwood roots by Navajo, Zuñi, and Hopi artisans. To many casual collectors and tourists, the kachinas — some of which may have been manufactured in Hong Kong or Taiwan — are simply pretty curios or decorative pieces to be placed in their chic southwestern-style homes or offices.

To the native people who believe in the living spirits of the Kachinam, the meaning is so much more. For the Hopi of northeastern Arizona, kachinas are the spirit essence of literally everything in the Hopi world. They serve as an expression of the Hopi people's bond with the earth, and an inspiration for the preservation of their culture and way of life.

In the gray months of winter when the earth slumbers, the first kachinas leave the San Francisco peaks and make their appearance at the Hopi mesas. They visit the cozy kivas, or underground temples, below the cold earth. As the seasons evolve and warm winds return, the Kachinam emerge and are seen in the village, just like the crops and other signs of new life. When the seasons change once again, the kachinas return to the peaks and the gods, carrying back the good-will of the mortals below, and word of the continuation of life. Kachinas remain the link among the native people and their deities and the earth which gives everyone so much.

But not all kachinas are necessarily good. Neither are all the gods. Along with the newer civilizations which have crept into the lands of the West come the gods of greed, consumption, indifference, and waste. They do not dwell in the snow-kissed peaks where winds are born, but they thrive in the urban sprawl of Phoenix, Las Vegas, Los Angeles, and other cities that suck the lifeblood from earth and rivers. These sinister gods dispatch the kachinas that we have come to fear and loathe — those towering kachinas of steel that march across the deserts, plains, and over the mountains. In their ugly iron clutches, these kachinas carry thick cables filled with electricity — power stolen from the land and the heavens — energy needed to fuel the mushrooming cities that only demand more and more and give nothing in return.

Thankfully, other kachinas are appearing on the landscape. These kachinas do not rob from the earth, but they help to power cities and towns by reaping the wind. Despite the hostilities of powerful utility companies and lobbyists who fear that their monopoly is threatened, pioneers in the wind-power industry have made inroads in California, on the high plains of Texas, and in other pockets of the West where wind is in abundance.

Out on the Texas Panhandle, just west of the town of Alanreed and near Jericho, our friends Delbert and Ruth Trew have erected giant wind turbines on ranchland that now serves also as a wind farm. The wind systems can produce thousands of valuable kilowatt-hours for a fraction of the cost. Angle-iron towers rise 150 feet in the air, and the propellers are seventy-five feet in diameter. Huge turbines turning wind into energy appear as larger versions of the wooden windmills that became weathered icons of the West's distant past — simple marvels of engineering that coaxed precious water from the earth.

"We have high hopes," Delbert told us when work crews started to erect the first test equipment on his ranch. "I hope Ruth and I will get to spend some of the royalty money those wind machines will produce." We hope so too. But even more than that, we look forward to the day when we can drive through the West and not see any more of those long lines of marching giant steel kachinas, but only whirling wind machines.

The answer my friend
is blowing in the wind,
the answer is blowing in the wind.

— Peter, Paul and Mary
"Blowing in the Wind"

Law West of the Pecos

The self-proclaimed title of Judge Roy Bean, ca. 1825-1903, a notorious frontiersman, saloon keeper, and Texas justice of the peace.

▪

Judge Roy Bean was a songdog tailor-made for Texas. Only that big brash state could get away with conjuring up a colorful figure of Bean's proportions. It is too bad we'll never know the truth, the whole truth, and nothing but the truth about this Kentucky native. What we do know is that Bean became a bona fide legend in his own time in the whistle-stop town of Langtry, where he was appointed justice of the peace in 1882 at the insistence of Texas Rangers trying to keep order along the wild Texas border. We also know that Bean named the town and his saloon after the famed English actress Lillie Langtry, known far and wide as "the Jersey Lily."

Although Bean was an unabashed racist and a greedy swindler, any culprit dragged before him could at least count on a speedy trial, nothing like the cumbersome

THE JERSEY LILY
ICE BEER
JUDGE ROY BEAN NOTARY PUBLIC

judicial proceedings of the future. The crusty old man dispensed his own brand of justice about as fast as he did ice-cold beer and shots of whiskey from his saloon-courtroom on the banks of the Rio Grande.

With the help of dime novelists and, later, Hollywood, Bean was vaulted to hero status, like so many other frontier rascals and eccentrics such as Davy Crockett and Calamity Jane. It is hard to separate fact from fiction, but the yarns live on — such as the story that Bean held an inquest over a dead man found with forty dollars and a pistol in his pockets.Bean promptly fined the corpse forty dollars for carrying a concealed weapon.

Bean, part history and part folklore, kept a pet bear he called Bruno, convinced a hung jury to get unhung by threatening the jurors with jail, and, in 1896, staged the forbidden world heavyweight championship between Peter Maher and Bob Fitzsimmons on a Rio Grande sandbar because prizefighting was illegal in Texas and Mexico.

Ironically, Bean died in 1903, too soon for him to meet his beloved Lillie Langtry. Less than a year after his death, she finally arrived in the town that bore her name, where the locals presented her with one of Bean's six-shooters and a plaque that read, "It aided him in finding some of his famous decisions and keeping order West of the Pecos River. It also kept order in the Jersey Lilly [sic] Saloon. Kindly accept this as a small token of our regards."

Wiping a tear from her eye, Miss Langtry graciously accepted the mementos, ordered a round of drinks for everyone in the saloon — and avoided having to adopt Bean's pet bear when Bruno broke his tether and sent everyone running.

Levi's

A trademark name for trousers of heavy denim, first manufactured in San Francisco in about 1853 at the peak of the gold rush by Bavarian immigrant tailor Levi Strauss. The first pants Strauss made were of heavy brown tent canvas. They could withstand the strain of bending, digging, and sifting in a riverbed for hours at a time. When his canvas supply dwindled, Strauss turned to a sturdy fabric manufactured in Nimes, France, called *"serge de Nimes."* Later, the name of this tough fabric was Americanized to *denim,* and patented copper rivets were used to keep pockets filled with gold from tearing. In a short time, every self-respecting miner and cowboy was wearing blue jeans — the quintessential American garment. Today, Levi's remain an international symbol of western culture and a definite fashion statement. As the time-honored saying goes, "Old Levi's never die. They just fade away."

▪

In 1977, while serving as a capital bureau chief for a chain of Texas newspapers, I went to meet a friend at the historic Driskill Hotel in downtown Austin and was barred from entering the bar because I was wearing Levi's. The young man greeting patrons explained with obvious disdain that the hotel's lounge had a new dress code. Denim pants, no matter how venerable the manufacturer, were no longer appropriate at this establishment, and guests wearing them would have to take their trade elsewhere.

I was caught completely off guard. My blue jeans were clean and looked much more presentable than the rumpled trousers worn by the self-important doorkeeper. Despite my protests, he stood his ground and called for reinforcements. Seeing that I was outmanned when a pair of gorillas with size-twenty necks loomed in the doorway, I summoned my friend. We beat a retreat to a nearby watering hole where our Levi's were accepted. But before we departed, I vowed loud enough for all to hear that I would return wearing my jeans. My cry, "Remember the Driskill!" echoed down the street.

There I was in Austin — capital of the Lone Star State — and refused service at a hotel that had acted as the city's social and political hub ever since a cattle baron first opened the place on Brazos Street back in 1886. And all because I wore a pair of Levi's.

Earlier that evening, I had found a spot at a Formica table and enjoyed a chicken-fried steak and a longneck Shiner's at Threadgill's, an old 1930s gas station converted to a roadhouse where Janis Joplin used to sing for her supper. Austin had several other great hangouts — the Broken Spoke, Liberty Lunch, the Raw Deal, the Texas Chili Parlor, and the legendary Armadillo World Headquarters — and all of them allowed customers to enter clad in denim. Fact is, it would have seemed kind of strange not to see people wearing blue jeans at these popular places.

I was still fuming over the Driskill incident the next morning while I drove down Congress Avenue to the capitol, the striking edifice of native pink granite built in the late 1880s by convict labor gangs. By the time I strode into the cavernous rotunda, I had a strategy clearly in mind. I made a beeline for the office of Pike Powers, a young attorney from Beaumont and the one legislator whom I thought could best remedy the odd malaise that ailed the Driskill by causing management to unleash its cockamamy ban on blue jeans.

Powers was horrified when I related my tale. After discussion, he summoned his top aide and, with a wink, promised me they would right this wrong quicker than I could say "Levi Strauss."

The result was the drafting of House Bill 2020, which called for making blue jeans "the official state costume" of the sovereign state of Texas. The proposed legislation further declared that it would be a misdemeanor for any public establishment in the state to refuse service to anyone wearing jeans — except in Austin, where such a grievous offense would be considered a felony. I lobbied hard to make it a hanging offense, but the Powers said that might be pushing it a bit too far.

Unfortunately, the proposed legislation did not even make it out of committee to get to the full House of Representatives for a vote. Thus a potentially important Texas law withered and died. But the resulting publicity about the controversy and the effort to make jeans respectable at the Driskill did not go unnoticed.

A few weeks after the confrontation at the hotel, I returned as promised, wearing my very best pair of Levi's. I was greeted at the door by the same young man, only this time he too was clad in blue jeans. He grinned as wide as the door he held open for me. I stepped inside to join a gang of blue-jean celebrants who in one voice bellowed loud enough to wake Levi Strauss from the dead, "Remember the Driskill!" There is a God after all, I thought to myself, and no doubt he wears Levi's 501 jeans.

Low Riders

A term used in the Hispanic West since World War II to describe both a vehicle that has been customized and lowered to the ground and the person who is driving it. Centered in southern California, particularly in the East Los Angeles and San Jose areas, the low-riding phenomena has spread to cities and small towns throughout Arizona, Texas, and New Mexico.

▪

We watch them as they rumble out of

the darkness in gleaming Fords, Pontiacs, and Mercuries. Mostly, they pick Chevies. All the cars are flawless — there is not a cull in the pack. They cruise the streets listening to tunes — oldies but goodies — with their motto, "low and slow," ever on their minds.

They are low riders on parade.

Low riding is a pride thing. Low and slow is the way to be.

— A low rider

During the 1940s, low riding originated in the tough barrios of Los Angeles, where gangs of *pachucos* in zoot suits lowered their cars by tossing bags of cement in the trunk. Low riding became a conscious rebellion against the stereotypical hot-rodding middle-class Anglo youth of the 1950s, as personified by James Dean. Times and customs changed. The pachucos are called cholos or *vatos locos* (crazy guys), but the pride and defiant attitude remain.

You travel from Texas to Arizona to New Mexico, or any state where there is 'Raza,' and you begin to notice that low riding has spread like wildfire. Every city has its cruising, where on weekends the boulevard comes to life. But low riding isn't just cruising. It's a movement.

— A low rider

Low riders cherish their cars as much as their wives and lovers — maybe even more. Many of them have put thousands of dollars into their cars just to make them look good. They call their cars "rides" and give them names such as "Gypsy Rose," "Angel Baby," "In the Night," "Wild Cherry," "the Ghost," and "Ecstasy."

The low riders are primarily young to middle-aged Hispanics. Their passion is to transform beat-up heaps and resurrected jalopies into vehicles with style and

elegance. Low riders' dreams are made of chrome and vinyl. They shear off the front coil springs so the sleek ride hugs the pavement. Inside, snug with his woman and with a longneck beer nestled between his knees, the low rider slinks low in the front seat, almost out of sight, and leaves the barrio for a fantasy drive in the summer dusk.

Low riding is not squealing tires or just being macho at the burger stand. It is a pride thing. That's what the low riders themselves will say. They prove it every time they go out on a ritualistic cruise. An integral part of the Mexican-American culture, low-ride caravanning has been compared by some sociologists to the Hispanic custom of men and women strolling, always in opposite directions, around the plaza — the center of activity in every town and city in the Southwest and Mexico. Group cruising — sometimes called "slow prancing" — is seen as a method of courting, a way for staking out territory, or simply a pleasant family activity.

When we first got married, my husband spent all his time working on the cars and I wasn't interested. But that changed. Now I'm into it too. These days the whole family — even the dog — cruises. Almost every night we work on our van called 'the Tear Drop Machine,' and on Sundays we cruise. We meet other families

at the car wash and then we cruise all afternoon and have a big dinner. It's a real family affair.

— A low rider's wife

No matter the reason for low riding, a must for any good ride is a hydraulic lift system with controls on the dashboard. This can make the front wheels hop off the pavement. At low-rider shows, champion "hoppers," looking for a cash prize or trophy, can make their rides leap two feet in the air.

We have seen low riders in L.A., San Jose, Tucson, Phoenix, El Paso, and Albuquerque. But our favorite place for observing the comings and goings of some of the most dedicated caravanners is Española — a northern New Mexican town in Rio Arriba County that has become a low-rider haven, twenty-five miles northwest of Santa Fe. Low riders can be seen there most any time of day or night. If you want your fill of low riders, go to Española on Friday or Saturday night or, better yet, on Sunday afternoon. Find a good vantage point at the Sonic Drive-In or at Blake's Lotta Burger, and prepare to witness a steady stream of classic rides cruising the highway from north to south. The only trouble low riders have is when the police stop them — not for speeding, but for going too slow.

One of the standard jokes around town goes, "How do you know when it's winter in Española? When the fur on the low riders' dashboards grows longer." Low riders are such a part of the local landscape that the chamber of commerce once even bought advertising space in national magazines, showing a hopping low rider with the message, "I've visited the Eiffel Tower and seen the Taj Mahal by moonlight, but it wasn't until I came to Española that I saw a '55 Chevy doing a mating dance."

In the low-rider capital or wherever else good rides cruise into the twilight, low and slow is the way to go.

It's pretty hard to explain how I feel about low riding. I've got years and years and about twelve thousand bucks in my '57 Chevy. It is my pride and joy. I love low riding. This is my life. I've been doing it since I was twelve years old. Before that I dreamed of it.

— A low rider

Marlboro Man

A fictitious cowboy who resides in a make-believe locale called Marlboro Country ("Behind every good story, there's a man who has lived it. Come to Marlboro Country"). This machismo masculine figure with chiseled good looks is used in extensive advertising campaigns by Philip Morris, Inc., to sell cigarettes.

■

Just like boots and saddles, Roy and Dale, or bows and arrows, cowboys and cigarettes have always seemed to go together. We understand this all too well after spending years wading through smoke-clogged beer joints, honky-tonks, and saloons across the West.

Where would that Old West we all know and love be without the vision of an inviting campfire next to a chuck wagon out on the lone prairie, with only the sounds of a harmonica and Spanish guitar duet, a songdog singing its heart out to the moon, and some stoved-up old cowpoke hacking up blood and guts thanks to a lifetime of inhaling "coffin nails"?

Sucking tobacco smoke into our lungs, snuffing it up noses, and chawin' on plugs and twists of the stuff were acquired habits in this country soon after the tobacco business boomed in colonial Virginia in the 1620s. English colonists taught Indians about the delights of their firewater and the Indians gave the whites their *tubak*.

Some years later, the mountain men, trappers, and sodbusters who migrated westward brought along their pipes, pouches of tobacco, and "stogies" — a cigar favored by freighters on Conestoga wagons.

After the Civil War, along with a great increase in the tobacco use, the most famed of all western smoking products appeared — Bull Durham. All over the American West, anyone who used smoking tobacco carried the little muslin sacks with a round tag dangling from the end of a drawstring and some "bibles" — slang for a cowboy's book of rolling papers.

Today, even though most smokers use tailor-made cigarettes, we still see that image of a rugged western male puffing on a smoke or dipping into a sack of Red Man or a tin of snuff to get a pinch. Although that Marlboro Man look is universal, it definitely applies to all the macho occupations of the American West — logger, miner, trucker, lawman, and oilfield roughneck.

Still, the one picture that will always persist is of a buckaroo on horseback rolling up a smoke with his one free hand, as he prepares to pop a kitchen match with his thumb. All the while, he squints into the dying sunset.

SURGEON GENERAL'S WARNING:
Quitting Smoking Now Greatly Reduces serious Risks to Your Health

Mirage

An illusion of land or water where none exists, a mirage (from the Latin word *mirare*, meaning "to look at") usually appears near the horizon and is caused by the nonuniform atmospheric refraction of light. The most common type of mirage is the oasis, or water mirage, that has deceived so many desert travelers. The word is often used figuratively for something that appears falsely to be real.

▪

It was in the high desert of Arizona just across the New Mexico border. We were traveling west as far as we could go, all the way to the Pacific shore. Our vehicles of choice for this particular adventure were a blue van filled with ice chests and the songs of Woody Guthrie and the Eagles, and in the lead a ragtop Corvette, as red as spilled blood, that had rolled off the assembly line in 1964.

Bitter coffee and greasy Gallup breakfasts churned in our stomachs, and we stayed thirsty all the time. Bottled water and a sack of shriveled peaches and grapes helped a little. Those riding in the van sucked in waves of cool air pouring from the dashboard vents. In the convertible, we tried to stay comfortable with damp bandannas — cowboy air conditioners — tied around our necks, and dreams of motel swimming pools that became real every evening. It was coming up on the Fourth of July, and there had not been any rain for a long time — just lots of sun and record-high temperatures that made front-page news all summer.

We passed a traditional Navajo hogan made of logs and earth, and saw a herd of sheep crowded into the slim ring of shade on one side of the dwelling. At the state line, we paused at Chief Yellowhorse, a stucco tepee trading post, to look at the neat rows of steer skulls baking in the desert heat. As usual, some tourists — this time a family from Arkansas — inspected the vintage Corvette. We bid them adieu and took to the road. The towns of Lupton, Allentown, Houck, Sanders, and Chambers came and went. Despite the strong sun, it was a gentle ride. Like desert creatures, we were adjusting to the climate.

Then off to the right, we spied the graveyard. At first it appeared to be an illusion, our eyes tricked by the hot air near the surface of the earth. But we slowed down and saw that it might be real. Without anyone saying a word, we turned around and went back. We stopped the van and the Corvette in swirls of cinnamon-colored dust to pay our respects to those we never knew.

There was a simplicity to the cemetery — no mausoleums, no bronze gates, no granite obelisks. There were no marble angels and lambs with fancy curls, no elaborate tombstones shipped from Saint Louis. The graveyard had a natural beauty without relying on manicured lawns and paths trimmed with ivy.

We realized that this was consecrated

ground. It was a *campo santo* — a blessed field. For twenty minutes, it became our oasis. Simple crosses marked many of the graves. The wood was weathered, and the inscriptions had been erased by too many seasons of dry winds and blowing sand. Now, only those who came on Memorial Day to pull up brittle grass, brush away tumbleweeds, and leave jars of wild blossoms knew for sure who rested there. Survivors returned on special dates such as feast days and birthdays and anniversaries. They usually came around Christmastime to festoon the graves with plastic poinsettias and garlands from Wal-Mart.

As we walked among the dead, none of us spoke very much. The strong hot wind blew away our words, and we stayed content with our thoughts. In our minds, we decided that it was an Indian cemetery. We found a grave with a handmade sign that could still be read, listing the name and years of the man buried below. A rubber Mighty Mouse doll, like a smiling cherub, was wired to the marker. Nearby, we stood over the grave of a man who had died too young. From the barely visible dates, we thought he had been a soldier in Vietnam. A china Madonna, intact except for her face, guarded the grave. We stood there and, as the living always do, passed judgment over the dead. We guessed that probably not a person buried there had ever uttered a line of *Hamlet* or gazed at a Cézanne or listened to a single phrase of Handel.

But as we turned to leave, we choked on our presumptions. We realized that in the silent dirt were people who had been given other gifts. They had been enraptured by the oral literature of elders who tended sheep and molded pottery and wove rugs that were works of art. They had watched thousands of sunsets that no one could ever capture on film or canvas. They had memorized the poetry of the coyote's song. The eternal wind was their benediction.

Back on the road, we stayed quiet for many miles. Then without warning, the hot wind vanished and the sky changed color. A cool rain fell and broke the earth's fever. We left the top down on the Corvette and opened the van's windows. The steady rain stayed with us the rest of the day as we raced on.

That evening, around yet another motel pool, we toasted the dying day with glasses of water cold enough to make us shiver. Even though the graveyard we had visited was on the beaten path, we were not certain we could ever find it again. Perhaps it had been only a mirage after all.

But inside the motel room was an ashtray holding highway treasures. Mixed with the souvenir fragments of concrete from the Mother Road, the old buckle and buttons dug from the pavement, the bits of animal bone, and the cafe matchbooks was a piece of glass we had found buried in the dust. It appeared to be a tiny Madonna's face. Her painted eyes were closed and there was just the trace of a smile. She was our best gift. She was the most revered of all our totems. It was Christmas in July. Our mirage was truly real.

Mojave

A desert covering more than twenty-five thousand square miles, mostly in southeastern California, south of Death Valley and the Sierra Nevada Mountains, and extending from the San Bernardino and San Jacinto mountains east to the Colorado River. Characterized by barren ranges, deep valleys, dry washes, salt flats, and shifting sand dunes, the Mojave averages less than five inches of rainfall annually.

▪

The old man appeared right around high noon, just on the brink of California's great Mojave desert. A wreath of snowy whiskers rimmed a face carved by time. Footprints left by generations of crows framed turquoise eyes brimming with wisdom. The man's worn and dusty clothing, cowboy hat, and boots had fused with his body.

He arrived from out of nowhere in an automobile, its color faded away by sun and sand. The dented dashboard served as an ashtray. Smoldering pipe remnants shrouded the old-timer's head like thick incense, giving him the appearance of a grizzled priest celebrating High Mass.

The old man and his car materialized next to a convenience store where we had paused to sip cool drinks and buy sacks of precious ice. Our departure from frenzied L.A. was already a memory, and we were prepared to streak across the quiet desert.

"Are ya havin' a good day?" the old man asked. We allowed that we were, but before we could ask the man about his own day, he beat us to the punch. "I drank curdled milk this morning," he told us. "I went into a grocery store and bought a half-gallon of milk and when I was driving down the highway I tilted the carton back and it was as sour as green apples. That was quite a surprise. But ya know, that isn't the worst thing that's ever happened to me. Sometimes it's good to get a little curdled milk. To experience the unexpected is the best gift of all."

The old man's smile was warm. Then he was gone; only the scent of his tobacco remained.

We climbed back into our car and crossed the Mojave. As always, it felt as though we were at sea. All day long, we encountered the best of the desert — the unexpected. We saw a pretty waitress behind the glass at the mythical Baghdad Cafe, an old ranch woman nodding her smiles from the wheel of a trusty pickup, and our friend Buster Burris headed for home in Amboy toting a rifle and sack of ice. In the midst of the Mojave, not far — as the buzzard flies — from where "Blood and Guts" Patton trained his desert warriors, we passed a man decked out in a dark business suit with wingtip shoes, strolling down the shoulder of the road like a stockbroker headed for a lunch date. Miles from even a ghost town, we were shocked to see a taxi cab whiz past with its roof lights on and a fare sitting in the back reading a newspaper.

Later, we stopped to stretch our legs on a length of desert highway flanked by a narrow berm of sand where the names and initials of passing travelers had been formed with rocks, cans, car parts, and other roadside debris. We spotted a peace symbol from the 1960s and a few solitary destinations such as *L.A.* and *Mexico* spelled out with sticks and stones. It was as though desert wayfarers had wanted to leave part of themselves behind and let others know they had passed this way.

We chewed down the rest of our melting ice and recalled favorite episodes of *Death Valley Days,* the long-running radio and, later, television western anthology about early desert pioneers. We remembered that it had been sponsored by Twenty Mule Team Borax and hosted at different times by Robert Taylor, Dale Robertson, Merle Haggard, and Ronald Reagan, before he gave up an acting career to become a politician. But we decided our favorite narrator was Stanley Andrews as "the Old Ranger."

Beyond the town of Needles, where it always has seemed pointless to own a thermometer, we made a twilight crossing over the Colorado River into Arizona and watched the Mojave disappear in the rearview mirror. It was dark when we slipped off the highway to pause at a service station where night birds chased moths flittering in the lights around the gas pumps. A sailor in his white uniform was on the pay phone letting the world know he was coming home, and a bowlegged cowboy came outside with a carton of sweet milk. He poured some into an upturned Frisbee, and in a heartbeat, a litter of half-grown cats danced out of the shadows and lined the rim of the makeshift saucer.

Throughout the rest of that summer and fall, there would be other cruises, more adventures, and new friendships forged. But images of that spring day and night, of sour and sweet milk, sun and shadows, out in the Mojave were some of our very best and most unexpected gifts.

Mountain Men

Name given to the rugged individuals who blazed trails into the Rocky

Mountains to trap beaver and hunt game from 1810 to 1840.

▪

Listen, ol' hoss, you ain't no pork-eater. So, mind your hair. After the rendezvous blowout and you had enough of the doin's and yer fill of Touse Lightnin,' keep your eyes skinned on the trail to the bull boat. I ain't worried 'bout Ol' Caleb gettin' you, but I am scared of you gettin' rubbed out by some hair-lifter or a white Indian who sure as shootin' is so grease-hungry that he goes after yer possibles bag and hairy banknotes and slices yer gullet with a frog-stabber.

— Mountain man, ca. 1820

Hey, man, you're no city slicker. So, watch your ass. After the Sierra Club picnic and you've had enough trail mix and your fill of Bud Light, be careful on the trail to the Jeep Cherokee. I'm not worried about an extraterrestial getting you, but I am fearful of you running into some biker or a militia member having such a Big Mac attack that he or she goes after your Eddie Bauer backpack and credit cards and blows you away with an assault rifle.

— Hiker, ca. 1995

A unique breed of self-reliant loners who called themselves mountain men, roamed the mountains of the West during the first half of the nineteenth century seeking highly prized beaver pelts to be used for fashionable hats in the eastern United States and Europe. When sartorial tastes changed and silk top hats became popular, the price for beaver skins fell sharply. By 1840, the demand had come to a halt. But the damage had been done. The semiaquatic rodents, known for their remarkable engineering feats, were almost extinct.

It took decades for this industrious species of animal to recover, but the mountain men never did. During their brief but colorful heyday, these hardy and daring trappers faced danger and often death on a daily basis. Typically clad in fringed buckskin suits decorated with dyed porcupine quills and colored glass beads, they often took Indian wives, for companionship and as a means of survival. Spending most of their time in the wilderness, mountain men made a point of gathering annually at a rendezvous site. For several weeks, they traded goods, renewed supplies, gambled, drank, feasted, and swapped stories of their great adventures.

Several mountain men merit special mention, especially those who went on to win fame as explorers, advancing the white American frontier.

▪

Kit Carson (1809-1868). Consummate frontier scout and Indian killer as well as a rancher and cavalry officer, Christopher "Kit" Houston Carson started as an illiterate mountain man and trapper. He guided John Frémont and Stephen Watts Kearny, served as an Indian agent, and fought at the first battle of Adobe Walls. In his own lifetime, Carson evolved into one of the most legendary figures in the history of the American West. Many of Carson's biographers have depicted him as larger than life — a noble hero and virtuous daredevil who felt sorry for the Indians he pursued and decimated. We believe otherwise

▪

Jim Bridger (1804-1881). Trapper, frontiersman, and government scout, Bridger best epitomizes the mountain men, if for no other reason than that he outlived most of the others. Powerfully built, grizzled and garrulous, Bridger is best known for having been a member of the party that opened the Oregon Trail. "Old Gabe," as he was known to his friends, was the first white person to visit the Great Salt Lake. We believe that is only appropriate because this bigger-than-life folk hero was a master at spinning yarns, many of which were to be taken with a pinch of salt.

▪

Other salty characters we consider noteworthy include:

John Colter, referred to as the model mountain man;

Jedediah Strong Smith, unparalleled pathfinder, killed at age thirty-two by a Comanche war party along the Cimarron River;

Hugh Glass, who crawled alone through one hundred miles of hostile territory after having been crippled by a grizzly;

"Liver Eatin' " John Johnson, alias Robert Redford's *Jeremiah Johnson*, mostly remembered for having carried on a war of personal revenge against the Crow tribe after a raiding party killed his Indian wife and unborn child;

Jim Beckwourth, who, after years as a mountain man and frontier scout, earned the not entirely deserved moniker of "gaudy liar;" and

William Sherley Williams, better known as "Old Bill," who thought enough of his prowess as a mountain man to demand that under all circumstances the initials "M.T.," for "master trapper," be attached to his name.

Necktie Party

A hanging; in particular, a lynching.

▪

Once upon a time there was a little girl in Germany whose name was Mary. She was born in 1875, about the same time Crazy Horse and Sitting Bull and hundreds of other Sioux people were deemed "hostiles" by the United States government. But Mary and her many brothers and sisters had never heard of the great Indian chiefs. They would not learn about them until the family left Germany. That happened when Mary was still a very little girl. Her father died, and Mary's mother decided to bring her brood to America in hopes of improving their lives.

During the long trip across the Atlantic, Mary's mother met a man on the ship, and they soon fell in love. He was a widower and also had many children of his own. By the time the ship docked in New York, the man had married Mary's mother. Between them, they had fifteen children. Some of the children eventually returned to Germany; others went to different parts of the United States. Most of the ones who stayed there headed due west. One of the sons started a fruit orchard in the Pacific Northwest, and another one kept going west until he reached Australia, where he became a cattleman.

Eventually, Mary went with her mother and stepfather and some of the others to live in Kansas City. When they moved there, folks were still talking about Jesse James and how the fabled bandit had met his end at the hands of the Ford brothers, just up the road in Saint Joseph, Missouri.

Around the turn of the century, when she was a young woman, Mary moved to New Orleans to keep house for one of her brothers. His name was Johnny. He was an artist, and he had a studio not far from the French Quarter.

To occupy her spare time, Mary got together with several other young women, and they visited and made fancy silk neckties. They became so adept at making ties that a man offered to sell them for the young women, and they were able to make some extra money that way. One day, Mary and her friends got a wild notion. They wrote their names and addresses on slips of paper and stuffed the papers inside the ties before they were boxed up. That particular batch of neckties ended up crossing the Sabine River that separated Louisiana and the Lone Star State.

Sometime later, a cowboy, not long returned from having served as a soldier in the Second Texas Regiment in the Spanish-American War, rode into Ballinger, Texas, the town closest to his father's place. The young man's name was Bert M. Dorsey. He not only did a little bit of cowboying, but he also spent as much time as possible racing bicycles. He even won some prizes.

He was born in Texas on the seventh day of the first week of 1876 — a pivotal year in the American West. In the next several months after the young Texan's birth, George Custer and his entire command would end their lives at Greasy Grass; James Butler "Wild Bill" Hickok would be shot and killed while playing poker in Deadwood, Dakota Territory; and the James gang would attempt an ill-fated bank robbery in Northfield, Minnesota.

Bert Dorsey came from honest-to-God cowboy country. The Chisholm Trail passed right through the heart of Waxahachie, the seat of Ennis County, where Bert was born. It was said that young Dorsey could take up his sack of Bull Durham and his rolling papers — his "cowboy bibles" — and fashion a tightly rolled smoke with one hand while on horseback or racing his bicycle. He was mostly Irish; he was pure Texan.

Bert came to town that day to get ready for the wedding of one his kinfolk, and he needed a new necktie. He went straight to the local general store and picked out the most colorful tie there. As he was taking it to the clerk, a slip of paper fell out of the tie and fluttered to the floor. Bert picked it up and saw the name and address of a young lady. He was curious, and he wrote her a letter. She wrote him back. He wrote a second letter. A regular correspondence developed. Then Bert hopped an eastbound train and went to New Orleans to meet his pen pal. They hit it right off.

Mary and Bert married and lived in New Orleans and later in Fort Worth. From there, they eventually moved with their baby son to Saint Louis, to a house on Texas Avenue, where a daughter was born.

Bert Dorsey made a living as a painter. He was not a fine artist like Mary's brother Johnny, who ended up dying of fever in New Orleans. Bert painted signs and displays on store windows. He died in a veterans' hospital in Saint Louis in 1939, and was given a soldier's burial at the national cemetery at Jefferson Barracks. When he died, his Bull Durham and cowboy bibles were close at hand. Mary lived until 1964, and then she joined Bert and was laid to rest in the same grave.

For several years before she died, Mary had lived with her daughter and her family. They built a small apartment for Mary, attached to their home. Mary's grandson loved to visit with his grandmother. All he had to do was walk a few steps from his house to her apartment. He entered her world and was swept away.

Most afternoons, he would go there. He would sit in her rocker, and Mary would make him hats from the pages of the *Saint Louis Post-Dispatch*. Then they would sing old cowboy tunes and barracks ballads, and she would feed the boy shortbread cookies, cups of strong tea, and her endless procession of stories.

The James gang, Teddy Roosevelt and his bold Rough Riders, and so many others joined the boy and the old woman in that tiny apartment. They were *right there*. The little boy saw them. There were more. Each twilight, he could count on witnessing cavalry charges, cattle drives, and parades of boys clad in khaki, all thanks to the little woman who wove her words as well as she simmered odd concoctions of German and Creole cuisine on a hot-plate burner.

Best of all, an old soldier cowboy who liked to race bicycles used to appear in that apartment. He had been dead for some time, but Mary was able to make him seem alive. In that way, the little boy came to know his grandfather, a tried and true Texan named Bert Dorsey.

Mary would pull out her husband's soldier ribbons and bicycle medals. She kept them in a pretty wooden box that had been used to hold the silk ties she had made. The boy especially loved her story of how Bert found her name inside the silk necktie. He never grew tired of hearing her tell it, and each time she did, they would click their teacups and devour another round of cookies. It became their own special "necktie party," only no one was ever strung up.

Even after the boy grew to be a man, he sometimes tried to imagine what Bert Dorsey's voice had sounded like or how he had carried himself. Mostly, he thought of Bert when the young man was back in Texas — fertile ground for making unknown grandfathers into personal legends. Because of Bert Dorsey, whenever the young man went to Texas, he felt as though he were going home. But he also thought about Bert and Mary when he pulled out an old wooden box. It was long and narrow, ideal for holding silk neckties.

▪

In both of our families, stories have been passed down from generation to generation, handed over like heirloom china or antique quilts. Many of the stories that nourished Michael as a boy growing up in Missouri came from his mother's mother, Mary Dorsey.

O.K. Corral

No single incident is more symbolic of the mythical Wild West than the fabled gunfight at the O.K. Corral. The brief but deadly confrontation took place on October 26, 1881, in Tombstone, Arizona, when town marshal Virgil Earp, along with recently deputized brothers Morgan and Wyatt and family friend Doc Holliday, confronted the Clanton and McLaury brothers alongside a vacant lot on Frémont Street near the O.K. Corral.

▪

WILD WEST JUDAICA

Full-length photographic portrait. Approx. 11½ x 5 inches. Very minor crease and scratch. Lightly tinted. Attractively archivally framed and glazed.

We are pleased to offer a spectacular photograph of Josephine Sarah Marcus Earp, the wife of frontier folk-hero Wyatt Earp. This is surely one of the most memorable photographs of a 19th-century American woman in existence. "Josie" Earp was a legendary beauty and a most unusual Jewish frontier wife. She met Wyatt Earp in Tombstone, Arizona in 1880, two years before the shootout at the O.K. Corral, and remained with him until his death in 1929. Their life together included residences in almost every legendary western frontier boom town from Mexico to Alaska.

This photograph (and the example we sold several years ago) bears unobtrusive markings suggesting that Mrs. Earp's image fell into the hands of novelty photography merchants in the early part of this century. A blurred and cropped reproduction of this great photograph is included as the frontispiece and jacket illustration of her fascinating biography, I Married Wyatt Earp.

When we catalogued another print of this beautiful image a number of years ago, it was the most ordered item we have ever handled: this record has not been surpassed. It is an extraordinary example of photographic Americana.

— *Rare-book and photograph catalog*, 1994

Wyatt and Josie Earp — now there was a love story that is hard to beat! Fact is, we consider it the greatest love story to come out of the Old West. It far outshines what we know about George and Libbie Custer, the tales of Judge Roy Bean and his well-publicized obsession with Lillie Langtry, those yarns about Belle Starr and her many lovers, or the legend of "Wild Bill" Hickok and "Calamity Jane." The Earps' romance may even be more enduring than the tragic relationship of Colorado silver baron Horace Tabor and his Baby Doe, or the lengthy marriage of the trick-shooting sensation Annie Oakley and Frank Butler.

Certainly the story of Wyatt and Josie Earp is far more interesting than all the accounts of Earp as a law officer, especially the story of that twenty-eight-second gun battle at the O.K. Corral.

Regardless of the revisionist theories, half-truths, and lies surrounding the O.K. Corral and the Tombstone period, the truth is — no matter how effective or ineffective he was when it came to keeping the peace — only about a half dozen of Wyatt Earp's almost eighty-one years on earth were devoted to law enforcement.

Of more interest to us is what happened to the illustrious Earp during the rest of his life with Josie — those many years they spent roaming the West together, from the Mojave to Alaska, while Wyatt worked as a gambler, miner, and saloon keeper. Few people know that for nearly a half-century after the dust had settled at the O.K. Corral, Earp carried on a love affair with Josie, the spirited Jewish woman who never left his side.

Josie's sense of adventure was quite evident from the start. Only fifteen years old when she ran away from her prosperous parents' home in San Francisco, Josie ended up in the wild reaches of Arizona Territory as part of a theatrical troupe performing Gilbert and Sullivan's *H.M.S. Pinafore.* She quickly was retrieved by her worried parents, but Johnny Behan, an Arizona lawman and politician, smitten with Josie, went to San Francisco and asked for her hand in marriage. She returned to Tombstone with Behan, not only a sheriff but also an Earp political rival and a good friend of the Clantons. In Tombstone, she first encountered Earp, who was a deputy sheriff and the proprietor of the Oriental Saloon. Josie's flaming romance with Behan quickly burned out, and Earp's marriage to his second wife, Mattie, was already on the rocks. Soon after meeting, Wyatt and Josie were embroiled in a love affair that lasted the rest of their lives.

On that famous day of the big shoot-out, Josie was close enough to hear the gunshots when the fracas erupted not far from the O.K. Corral, leaving Billy Clanton and Tom and Frank McLaury dead, three others wounded, and only Ike Clanton and Wyatt Earp unscathed. In the aftermath of the O.K. Corral, Josie stuck by her man and the actions he had taken in that quick but deadly street fight, which dogged Earp for the rest of his life.

Some writers who follow Earp's wanderings claim that no legal document attesting to their marriage exists, but Josie and Wyatt lived as husband and wife for nearly fifty years. Most of those who knew the couple were at a loss to explain how they managed to stay together so long, because they seemed so different from each other. Earp was quiet and reserved, but his wife came off as fiery and temperamental. One family member was even quoted as saying, "You can't tell me that Wyatt was a killer . . . he lived with Josie for fifty years!" Still, the fact remains that Josie followed Earp wherever he went and remained a devoted wife to the very end.

For Earp, the end came in Los Angeles, just a few minutes past eight in the morning on January 13, 1929. The old lawman died quietly. As Josie later wrote in her published recollections, "My darling had breathed his last, dying peacefully, without a struggle, like a baby going to sleep. I don't know how long I continued to hold him in my arms; I wouldn't let him go. They finally had to drag me away. I had gone with him on every trail he had ever taken since those days at Tombstone so long ago."

Josie was too shaken to attend the funeral services at Pierce Brothers' Chapel in Los Angeles. Included among Earp's honorary pallbearers were cowboy movie heroes William S. Hart and Tom Mix. Later, Josie buried Wyatt's ashes in the Hills of Eternity, a Jewish cemetery in Colma, just south of San Francisco. When Josie died in 1944, she was laid to rest with her husband. There they will remain forever.

Almost every day, visitors come to the cemetery and find the simple grave with a single plaque marked only with the names of Wyatt and Josie and their birth and death dates. Some of those who come to pay their respects are cowboys. They doff their hats and stand there on the manicured grass, surrounded by tombstones topped with menorahs and Stars of David, a world away from the blood and smoke of the O.K. Corral.

101 Ranch

A legendary Oklahoma ranch founded in the late 1800s by George Washington Miller and maintained for many years by his three sons, Joe, Zack, and George. This ranch, which created many myths and colorful tales, was also an important agricultural enterprise, played a role in the development of the oil industry, and served as a spawning ground for Wild West shows and the fledgling western motion-picture business. Such film stars as Tom Mix, Hoot Gibson, Buck Jones, and Ken Maynard all drew paychecks from the 101. The ranch later fell on hard times and was sold off during the Great Depression, but in its glory years, such famous figures as Geronimo, Buffalo Bill Cody, Will Rogers, and hundreds of others spent time on the spread. Bill Pickett, the man who invented bulldogging, was one of the most beloved 101 Ranch cowboys.

■

There never was another cowboy quite like Bill Pickett. The world of brave bull riders, bronc busters, and steer wrestlers will never see his match. If anyone not drunk or crazy ever dares to wager otherwise, take the bet. Snap it up quick and raise the ante. That will be sure money in the bank.

Never mind that this cowboy was a black man subjected to extreme prejudice. Never mind that he was one of thirteen children born to dirt-poor former slaves. Never mind that he never got much formal schooling. Never mind that his earnings were most always far less than those paid to white men who were not half the ranch hand he was. In the long run, as far as the measure of the man goes, none of that means a damn thing except that the odds were against Pickett from the get go. But he still emerged a winner.

This cowboy who spent most of his professional career riding for the 101 Ranch invented bulldogging. That single act alone should be enough to ensure that Pickett will dwell forever in the hearts and minds of anyone who has the moxie and gumption to hold himself out as a rodeo cowboy — especially a bulldogger. Combination daredevil acrobat and brawny grappler, a bulldogger needs more nerves than sense just to stay alive — let alone make a decent living or walk away with a trophy belt buckle.

One of seven standard events in modern rodeo, bulldogging, or steer wrestling, consists of a rider jumping from his horse onto a running steer, then grabbing and twisting the animal's horns until it is brought to the ground. The performance is judged according to the time that elapses between the contestant's leaving the starting box and the exact moment when a field judge drops his flag to signify that the steer is down, with all its legs extending straight out.

Popular legend has it that while he was working on a cattle spread in central Texas, Bill Pickett unveiled his rather unconventional method of throwing a steer. Pickett was riding the range, minding a herd and his own business, when he saw an ornery steer charge hard from out of nowhere. It was clear that the steer was about to gore Pickett's horse. As the steer drew close to his mount, Pickett suddenly leaped from the saddle and grabbed the critter by the horns. Then he swiftly bent down, bit the steer's upper lip, and jerked his head, pitching the animal to the ground. Another wrangler rushed to Pickett's assistance and helped tie up the steer's legs. Thus was born the art of bulldogging — said to be the only rodeo event originated by an individual.

Soon after the incident with the wild steer in Texas, Pickett's boss decided that Bill should try his hand at show business. The hardworking Pickett became known throughout the country as the cowpoke who did bulldogging with his teeth. Finally, he brought his unusual style of steer wrestling to the Miller Brothers' 101 Ranch, in northern Oklahoma Territory.

Recruited by Zack Miller to appear with the 101 Ranch cowboys, Pickett made his debut at the 101 in June of 1905, when sixty-five thousand people showed up to attend the convention of the National Editorial Association. The three Miller brothers, riding abreast at the head of an endless parade of cowboys and cowgirls, a complete cavalry musical band, and the Apache chief Geronimo, followed by two hundred Indians from a half-dozen tribes, were tough acts to follow — but not for Bill Pickett. Right after the staged buffalo hunt and the bronc riding were over, it was time for him to perform.

The announcer's voice boomed loud and clear through a megaphone: "Ladies and gentlemen, the next event will be Bill Pickett, the Dusky Demon from Texas, who will leap from the back of a running horse onto a running steer and throw the steer with his bare hands and teeth."

The audience gasped as the thousand-pound steer raced at full speed in front of the grandstand. Then Bill Pickett appeared. He was astride his bay horse named Spradley. In what seemed like an instant, Pickett was sliding off his speeding horse onto the huge steer's back. He grabbed a flashing horn in each hand, dug his high-heeled boots into the dirt, and twisted the steer's neck until his face was turned upward. Then Pickett's teeth gnashed on the steer's lip. The cowboy lifted his hands in the air and gave his body a twist. The steer fell on its side and lay perfectly quiet as Pickett rendered him helpless. As if one body, the huge crowd jumped to its feet. The roar of applause was said to be deafening. For Pickett, it had to be more delicious than beefsteak. It was only one of thousands of moments he savored during his action-packed life.

Pickett's "bite 'em on the lips" style of wrestling steers thrilled audiences at 101 Ranch events staged across the nation. He became a headline star as the 101 Ranch Wild West Show traveled the world. Pickett even tackled fierce fighting bulls before hostile crowds in Mexican bullrings.

At one encounter with a bull in Mexico City, Pickett managed to win an impossible — and sizable — bet for the Millers. The terms of the wager were that Pickett had to remain in the ring with the bull for at least fifteen minutes and spend five minutes with his hands on the bull's deadly horns. Although his beloved horse Spradley was gored badly (he recovered) and Pickett received wounds and bumps, including broken ribs, from a beer bottle flung from the stands, he held on for dear life — and won. He had remained in the arena for an amazing thirty-eight-and-a-half minutes, with seven-and-a-half of those minutes spent clinging to the bull's back and horns.

Pickett appeared in some western films and, for decades, kept up his bulldogging ways with the Millers, through lean and prosperous times. He was many things, but most of all Pickett was loyal. Even when the eventual demise of the 101 Ranch came about, with only Zack remaining of the Miller brothers, Pickett was right there at his side.

In March 1932, while he was trying to rope a half-broken horse, Pickett was badly kicked in the head. He was rushed to a hospital, but the old cowboy never regained consciousness. On April 2, after a two-week struggle, Bill Pickett died.

His funeral was held at the 101 Ranch, on the front porch of the Miller family home, called the White House. Indians, farmers, city folks, fans, and hundreds of cowboys and cowgirls showed up to say good-bye to Bill. Zack Miller wrote a poem about his friend. Zack called him the most faithful and the best cowboy who ever rode for the outfit. They laid Pickett to rest on a hill south of the ranch headquarters, not far from the grave of White Eagle, a Ponca chief who also had been a friend of the 101. Old-timers say Bill's horse Spradley is buried nearby.

Peacemaker

A popular name for the Colt Revolver Model 1873, the most famous handgun of the West. Much of the appeal of this six-shooter was because it used the same .44-caliber ammunition as the Winchester repeating rifle that first was manufactured the same year. Carried by lawmakers and lawbreakers, the Colt revolver came to be known as "the gun that won the West."

▪

"God did not make all men equal," old-time westerners were fond of saying "Samuel Colt did." We always thought it rather ironic that such a deadly weapon should get the name *peacemaker.* But then we also think it curious that so many Americans continue to tote guns. At least Old West gunslingers were required to check their weapons when they came to town. Not anymore — anyone is liable to be carrying a firearm.

With the coming to power of the National Rifle Association, arguably one of the most influential lobbying groups in the nation, all sorts of people — students, clergymen, PTA presidents — are packing guns.

We do not belong to the NRA — no way. No guns for us, not even the peacemaker. Our weapon of choice is the knife. To be even more specific, the bowie knife — a lethal weapon that is every bit as American as any gun ever made.

A versatile tool developed in the late 1820s, the bowie knife was standard equipment for frontiersmen throughout the American West. Most bowie knives had blades that ranged from nine to fifteen inches in length, with iron or brass guards to protect the hands.

Contrary to popular belief, the bowie knife was not invented by James Bowie (pronounced *boowie*), one of the mythicized heroes of the Alamo. He was, in fact, a land speculator, slave trader, and treasure hunter known through the tall tales surrounding him to be bold enough to rope and wrestle an alligator.

Tradition among aficionados holds that the first of these coveted knives was custom-made for Bowie by his brother Rezin Bowie. Another claim is that this celebrated piece of cutlery was created by Arkansas blacksmith James Black, hence the homespun nickname "Arkansas toothpick." Undoubtedly the work of many hands, the imposing knife with the curved, razor-sharp blade first became a prized collector's item of eastern dudes. But out west, the bowie knife remained part of the arsenal of

most self-respecting adventurers, who used it not only in close combat but also as an eating implement, to skin game, cut firewood, or even to dig a grave out on the lone prairie.

We agree with Texas newspaper columnist Molly Ivins in our push for every red-blooded American to carry a concealed bowie knife. Just think about it. You have to be in good shape to chase somebody down before stabbing your quarry, so the knife promotes physical fitness. Also, you never ever hear about people killing themselves while cleaning their knives — unlike guns.

Forget guns. They are for sissies. Give us an "Arkansas toothpick" any day. Maybe we will even start up our own association. Just let *them* try to take away our bowie knives.

Pickup

A type of truck with a cab for driver and passengers and a bed for hauling manure, bales of hay, barbed wire, or just about anything else.

■

Across the American West, the pickup truck has become the newest version of the trusty quarter horse. Ranchers aren't the only ones who prefer pickups. Peace officers, park rangers, lawyers, and accountants are consumed by the raging passion for "pick-'em-up" trucks.

Certainly anyone anywhere in the nation can own a pickup, but the drivers who look most comfortable behind the wheel are the cowboys and cowgirls — urban and rural varieties — who bounce along ranch and farm roads and cruise highways and boulevards west of the Mississippi. Like the rednecks from the Deep South whose transportation of choice is the pickup, the good ol' boy pickup drivers of the West are usually seen wearing "gimme" caps — but some still prefer a big cowboy hat with a full complement of handy toothpicks stuck in the hatband.

Standard equipment for the serious pickup driver includes a gun rack in the back window, a trailer hitch, a radio tuned to an AM country-western station, and a bumper sticker that's liable to proclaim anything from "Let's Rodeo" or "Eat More Beef" to "God Bless John Wayne" or "Custer Had It Coming."

Optional pickup features are National Rifle Association decals for hard-core gun toters, mud flaps, and oversized tires for drivers suffering from an Alan Ladd complex. Most pickups worth the price of an inspection sticker will have a dog — preferably a big one — riding in the back, a lukewarm six-pack on the front seat, and a foam cup to hold tobacco spittle.

We have never owned a pickup. But a long time ago, we had one of those vehicles that was not quite a pickup and not quite a car — sort of half and half. It was a pink and white Ford Ranchero with a truck bed, and a front half that was low and sleek like an automobile. We named it *El Coyote*, after our revered songdog.

El Coyote served us well. We used it for practical day-to-day trips to the store and laundromat. Whenever someone from our circle needed to move, we were able to help out in a big way. Best of all were the trout-fishing treks or our discovery of hidden destinations with the back end of *El Coyote* overflowing with friends and sleeping bags.

Everything was going well — and then we went and lost that hybrid pickup. Well, actually, we misplaced it. We parked it on a lonely road high in the Sangre de Cristos, and try as we might, we never could find it again. Last time we saw *El Coyote*, it was sitting there in the high-country sunshine with a half tank of gasoline, looking as content as a cow pony grazing in thick clover.

We like to think it's still there today.

Quicksand

Deep, loose, fine sand, saturated with water, that behaves like a soft mass and can become a dangerous and even deadly trap for animals or humans. Quicksand forms on sandbars, sand flats, and the bottoms of streams. Although the danger of quicksand has been exaggerated greatly, it should be approached with caution.

■

For a little kid glued to a western matinée, nothing was as frightening as a quicksand scene. Not crazed grizzly bears, not Jack Palance as the murderous hired gun in *Shane*, not even the most vile characters dreamed up by Sam Peckinpah struck terror in young hearts like a patch of quicksand. Crunched down in a theater seat watching some poor soul or critter get sucked to death in quicksand was pure torture. Even when a black-hatted villain was mired in the thick living soup, everyone felt a tinge of sympathy as the victim's outstretched hand, grasping at air, sank out of sight.

We all tried to imagine what it must be like to get stuck. We knew quicksand was not land, not water, but something in between. We also knew that being trapped in quicksand was like getting caught in a giant Chinese handcuff — the more you yanked, the greater the suction. The best method of escape, once you started to sink, was not to struggle but to position yourself on the surface and roll out — or grab the lariat pitched to you by some gallant hero on horseback who always appeared just in the nick of time.

The frightening stuff was here and there all along the banks, and often sucked at our feet in midstream as we waded across. The trick is to keep moving. When the surface is exposed to the air, quicksand, with a skin of surface tension on the top, is like cooled chocolate pudding. Move briskly enough and you can pass over the quaking skin without breaking it. Or you can play on it as on a trampoline, shifting your weight from one foot to the other while the whole mass shudders rhythmically back and forth under you. But if you play this way long enough, the skin will finally split, showing the darker, wetter jelly below. Then it is best to move rapidly, and find another game to play. Not that there is any real danger, of course. They say you always hit solid bottom before you sink out of sight. That's what they say.

— Jerome Doolittle
Canyons and Mesas

Remember the Alamo

Battle cry of the "Texian" rebels fighting for independence from Mexico. It came about as a result of the carnage sustained at the Alamo, the Franciscan mission built by the Spanish in 1718. Located in downtown San Antonio, Texas, the historic building evolved into a shrine famous for its role in the Texas revolt against Mexican rule.

▪

Most of us grew up believing the Alamo was where, in 1836, Colonel William B. Travis and 189 brave defenders, including frontier legends James Bowie and Davy Crockett, took a stand for ten days behind mission walls in a fight for independence against six thousand Mexican soldiers led by General Santa Anna. The deaths of that band of heroes, considered by most red-blooded Anglo Texans to be martyrs of liberty, resulted in the war cry — "Remember the Alamo!" — that rallied the rebellious Anglos and led to Texas becoming an independent nation known as the Lone Star Republic.

The story of what actually led to the siege of the Alamo, as presented by Texas writers and perpetuated by the Hollywood images of Fess Parker and John Wayne, needs to be reexamined. In truth, the three hundred American families brought to Texas by Stephen F. Austin in 1823 had swelled to thirty thousand within a decade, with few of these immigrants willing to abide by the terms on which settlement of Mexico's northern province had been encouraged. From the start, the colonists considered themselves Americans, not Mexican citizens, and openly showed their resentment to civil and church authorities. Worst of all, the newcomers brought thousands of black slaves with them, a blatant violation of the Mexican constitution.

The situation became grim in 1834 when Antonio López de Santa Anna became president of Mexico and was alarmed by what appeared to be the imperialistic expansion of the United States of America. Meanwhile, the colonists became weary of the many regulations and restrictions imposed by the Mexican government. These fears, cultural differences, and the issue of slavery led to the American settlers setting up a provisional government and ousting Mexican troops from San Antonio.

To restore order, in 1836, Santa Anna marched his army to San Antonio, where the now legendary siege at the abandoned mission called the Alamo began on February 23. It ended on March 6, when the Mexicans breached the walls and killed all the defenders except a few noncombatants.

Today, long after "Remember the Alamo!" ignited Anglo patriots to victory at the Battle of San Jacinto, a group of stalwart Texans still defends the Alamo and its image. The defenders are the Daughters of the Republic of Texas (DRT), an organization of women who trace their ancestors to Texas' years as a republic, from 1836 to 1845. Official caretaker of the Alamo since 1905, the DRT fights to preserve the Alamo legend and resists all attacks on this bastion of Texas pride.

Nonetheless, many historians and others, including many of the tens of thousands of Mexican Americans making up the population of the modern city of San Antonio, cannot help but view the Alamo not as an icon of liberty and sacrifice but more as a symbol of racism and imperialism.

Roadkill

Popular name for any wild or domestic creature — including mammals, birds, and reptiles — that has been struck or run over by a vehicle.

▪

Although we jokingly dubbed one of our tastiest chili recipes "Roadkill Chili" (a derivation of the prizewinning "Buzzard's Breath Chili," which calls for dead cow meat, dried red ants, and cigar ashes), it is always sad to see the smorgasbord of squashed critters strewn up and down ranch and farm roads of the American West. Some of them never even make it to the yellow stripes. It seems that even the speediest cannot outrun a semi or car that is going hell-bent for leather.

We've seen them all — jackrabbits, possums, deer, snakes, and turtles. Then, of course, there is one animal that seems to be the classic roadkill species — the armadillo.

Have you ever wondered about all those squashed armadillos you see on two-lane asphalt roads going to nowhere? Maybe you think they met their end because they were near-sighted. Not really.

In truth, armadillos often end up as roadkill because of an odd fright reflex that causes them to jump straight up if a moving vehicle passes over them. It's not the wheels that do the damage, but the self-inflicted injury that results when the armadillo hits the underside of a car or truck.

These odd-looking beasts with armor suits carved their own niche in the American West in the mid-nineteenth century when the nine-banded armadillo crossed the Rio Grande and took up residence in Texas. The "wetback 'dillos" joined with others who had escaped from roadside zoos or were unwanted pets turned loose. By the 1920s, the animals had crept into the Deep South. Today they range from Florida to New Mexico, but the heart and soul of armadillo country remains Oklahoma and especially Texas. The prehistoric mammals help sell beer, end up in high-stake races, chili pots, or as sausage, and, in 1981, were designated by Lone Star State lawmakers as the official state mascot.

Although published medical studies purport that some wild armadillos carry a form of leprosy, a good many westerners — some of them sporting armadillo boots — take issue with these claims and point out that any ailments armadillos might have are not contagious to humans. Diehard armadillo fans still revere these creatures that were nicknamed "Hoover hogs" during the Great Depression, when poor people resorted to eating baked 'dillos on the half shell to avoid starvation.

If only the armadillo could learn to do something about all that jumping.

Let's Rodeo

A slogan for a Texas boot manufacturer. Also, a popular cry in western barrooms and at arenas devoted to the sport of rodeo. The word *rodeo* comes from the Spanish *rodear*, to surround or encircle. In the Southwest, the rodeo was a roundup or gathering of cattle that evolved into a competition among cowboys and cowgirls of various skills originally developed from working cattle.

▪

Tens of thousands of fans still flock to the biggest and supposedly best rodeos around, from the Pendleton Roundup and Calgary Stampede to the big shows at Cheyenne, Fort Worth, and Houston's Astrodome, where — if you get a perch in the cheap seats — the rodeo arena looks like a postage stamp. Some people even prefer to witness rodeos at Madison Square Garden, in the wilds of Manhattan.

Not us. We still believe the most authentic rodeos are the small ones. That's where the true-blue fans go to see the real thing. We head to Bandera, Alpine, Shamrock, Taos, Flagstaff, or just about anyplace in the West where bronc riding, bulldogging, calf roping, and barrel racing can be watched up close and personal from wooden bleachers. Like so much else, rodeo has become big-time, big business, and big bucks. That's why we prefer to get our rodeo fix at little ranch burgs with dusty, sun-baked arenas. That's why we cling to memories of some of the all-time rodeo greats we were lucky enough to meet along the way.

There were bronc busters, hellfire cowgirl racers, and rodeo clowns without an ounce of fear in their hearts. All of them deserve a place in rodeo heaven, but for our money, the best we ever met was Warren Granger Brown, a bull rider known as Freckles.

Born on a Wyoming homestead in 1921, Brown learned to ride horses and herd cattle when he was a boy. By the time he was fourteen — living and working on an Arizona ranch — he picked up the nickname he carried for the rest of his days. "You could hurt your eyes trying to find any freckles on me now," he told us. "I reckon all those bulls I've been riding over the years just shook those freckles off."

He was sixteen when he rode his first bull in rodeo competition at Wilcox, Arizona. By the time he finally hung up his chaps and spurs in 1974, Freckles had earned a boxcar load of trophies, belt buckles, loving cups, engraved saddles, and prize money — and the admiration of rodeo fans throughout the world.

Freckles was a professional's professional, the cowboy's cowboy, and for an incredible thirty-seven-year span, a consistent winner. His litany of injuries included ten broken legs, two broken collarbones, countless broken ribs, and breaking his neck twice and his leg three times within a thirteen-month period.

In 1962, Freckles earned the coveted title "world champion bull rider" at the ripe old age of forty-one. Nobody, not even Freckles himself, knew just how many bulls and broncs he rode during his long and colorful career. In one two-day period, he climbed on forty-one bucking horses, and on more than one occasion he rode as many as twenty bulls in a day.

But in 1967, at the National Finals Rodeo in Oklahoma City, Freckles left his name permanently inscribed in the annals of rodeo history. That was when he tangled with a snorting beast that had defeated more than 220 cowboys and was considered to be the toughest rodeo bull ever to come out of a chute. The eighteen-hundred-pound Brahma was named Tornado, and no one had ever been able to make the eternal eight-second ride on the critter's broad back. When he drew Tornado, Freckles was a month shy of his forty-seventh birthday.

"It was the greatest experience of my life," Freckles told us years later. "I had never drawn Tornado before. I knew him, though. I'd watched him . . . and I knew I had to ride him. Many a cowboy said he couldn't be rode. A lot of guys would draw him and not even try to ride him. They would walk away. But I had to give him a go."

Freckles won. He beat Tornado. Some rodeo aficionados claim Freckles' Tornado ride was one of the finest events in rodeo history. When the five-foot-seven-inch, 150-pound cowboy left the arena that evening with tears in his eyes and Stetson in hand, he said to no one in particular, "He was overdue."

Freckles is dead, and the fighting bull named Tornado is buried at the National Cowboy Hall of Fame in Oklahoma City. Still, that eight-second dream for the rodeo champion lives on. So do the words the old bull rider told us when we asked him if he was happy with his life.

"All I ever wanted was to be a good cowboy," smiled Freckles.

And tonight bull ridin' histry's made,
a cowboy gained a crown
his bull was called Tornado
and the cowboy Freckles Brown.

— Red Steagall
"For Freckles Brown"

Santa Anna's Leg

ca. 1795–1876. Mexican general and President Antonio López de Santa Anna is best known by citizens of the United States for leading what has been perceived as a ruthless military campaign against Texas and massacring the captured defenders of the Alamo in San Antonio in 1836. He is sometimes called the "Napoleon of the West" or "Butcher of the Alamo," depending on the side of the border.

▪

Every so often, we throw a party to commemorate the anniversary of the burial of Santa Anna's leg. With mariachi tunes blaring, we serve succulent drumsticks, lay out our very finest tequila, and manage to produce a cake shaped vaguely like the old dictator's severed gam.

Instead of playing "Degüello," the Mexican hymn of fire and death that Santa Anna's band played at dawn on March 6, 1836, as the final assault on the Alamo was about to begin, we opt for a more appropriate fiesta tune — "The Yellow Rose of Texas." A minstrel song that existed before Santa Anna clashed with the Texas rebels, its refrain took on new meaning at the Battle of San Jacinto. A mulatto slave girl who had become the object of Santa Anna's desire managed to "detain" the general during his siesta, allowing Sam

Houston and his army to take their enemy by surprise and win Texas' independence from Mexico in a battle that lasted a mere eighteen minutes.

Our Santa Anna party is not intended to honor the infamous Mexican dictator for his role at the Alamo or his subsequent defeat at San Jacinto. We like to remind our revelers about other aspects of Santa Anna's colorful life — such as the state funeral he held for his forlorn leg, or the old rascal's esteemed place in the annals of chewing-gum history.

It seems that after Houston and his boys gave the Mexican army a good country licking at San Jacinto, the Mexican government and people repudiated their esteemed Santa Anna, and he went into exile in Cuba. By 1838, only two years after he had taken his leave, Santa Anna returned to Mexico to face invading French troops at Vera Cruz. He rode back into the limelight on his white charger, only to be shot out of the saddle by a French cannonball which shattered his leg below the knee. The loss of his limb in battle made Santa Anna something of a martyr, and it so revived his popularity throughout the country that in 1841, he again became president.

The following year, when sympathy for the one-legged dictator was reaching a peak, "His Serene Highness," as Santa Anna preferred to be called, staged what seemed like a continuous celebration to mark his birthday. The climax event was on September 27, when Santa Anna ordered his leg to be dug up at Manga de Clavo and brought to Mexico City. Cavalry, infantry, and artillery troops, as well as the cadet corps from the military academy at Chapultepec — all of them in full dress uniforms — escorted the urn bearing the grisly relic across the city to the magnificent tomb that had been erected in the cemetery at Santa Paula.

Dignitaries, including foreign ministers and diplomats, showed up to hear speeches and poetry. His Serene Highness solemnized the occasion by wearing a fancy new cork leg.

The fanfare soon died. By 1844, when another revolt occurred against his stern rule, Santa Anna was exiled for a second time. Nevertheless, Mexico's love-hate relationship with its mercurial leader continued. In 1846, he returned to lead the army against the United States in the Mexican War. Things quickly soured. In 1847, as some Illinois militiamen came upon his carriage, Santa Anna escaped on a mule, abandoning his half-eaten chicken lunch and his cork leg, covered with a calfskin boot. The Americans pounced on their unusual trophy and took it home with them.

Defeated in several more battles, Santa Anna again left Mexico, but was recalled in 1853 to serve as president for one year. After boldly proclaiming himself president for life, he was overthrown by reformists and fled the country in 1855. During the next couple of decades, he was in and out of Mexico. In 1863, during one of the periods when he was out of favor with his subjects, an angry mob removed Santa Anna's leg from the tomb in Mexico City, tied a cord around the stump, and dragged it through the streets. Later, some kind-spirited people took charge of the forlorn leg, and it was quietly buried again.

During the last few years of his life, Santa Anna was allowed to return to Mexico permanently. He died alone and mostly forgotten on June 21, 1876, just days before another major egotist — George Armstrong Custer — got his comeuppance at the Little Bighorn River.

A couple of footnotes (perhaps we should say legnotes) about Señor Santa Anna: Late in his life, Santa Anna brought a quarter-ton of tree resin called chicle to Staten Island, where he met with Thomas Adams Jr., who hoped to use the substance to create artificial rubber. That scheme failed, but in 1871 Adams began to market balls of unflavored chicle as chewing gum, just as it had been used for hundreds of years by some Indians tribes and folks from south of the border. After chewing gum-magnate William Wrigley Jr. unveiled his own brand, gum became popular throughout the nation and in Mexico, and is considered possibly Santa Anna's most important contribution to his country.

Meanwhile, despite some attempts to return it to Texas or Mexico, that well-traveled artificial leg — complete with boot — remained a treasured battle prize on permanent display at a small National Guard museum in Springfield, Illinois. But even though the coveted leg resided far from its owner's old stomping grounds, proud Texans finally recovered a valuable souvenir to remind them of their dreaded foe. In the late 1980s, the guardians of the Alamo took possession of the fancy brass cot that Santa Anna supposedly had shared with his favorite mistress — Melchora Iniega Barrera — as his soldiers overran that Shrine of Texas Liberty.

The beguiling Señorita Barrera, seventeen-year-old daughter of a prominent San Antonio widow, wed the already married Santa Anna after he had one of his sergeants, a thespian who spoke Latin, dress in priest's vestments and perform a mock ceremony to appease the girl's strict mother. Years later, in another strange historical twist, Santa Anna's bogus wife legally married the soldier who posed as a padre, allowing him to get a leg up on his former commander.

Santos

The Spanish word for *saints*, these handmade sacred images of saints or holy persons, found mostly in New Mexico, are fashioned from cottonwood by woodcarvers, or *santeros*. Wooden images carved in the round are known as *bultos*, and two-dimensional line paintings of saints, on flat boards, are called *retablos*.

▪

Our favorite santos are old friends. We cherish the retablos and bultos created by some of the best santeros of New Mexico, but we care just as much for the santos we have acquired from lesser known wood-carvers. All of them are equally important to us.

One of the carved wooden figures we favor the most was found during the hustle and bustle of the Spanish Market, held each summer in Santa Fe. The market was at its peak, and we were beneath the shade trees in the heart of the plaza park, examining the carvings laid out by the youngest exhibitors. A critical part of the effort to preserve traditional Hispanic arts and crafts and the culture of their ancestors, these children and teenagers were the descendants of some of the most respected santeros of old.

Some of the youngsters on the plaza came from families which have always kept a close relationship with the lay religious brotherhood found exclusively in the region. Known as *La Fraternidad Piadosa de Nuestro Padre Jesús Nazareno*, or the Pious Fraternity of Our Father Jesus the Nazarene, the members of this Hermandad, or brotherhood, are called *Los Hermanos Penitentes*, the Penitent Brothers, or simply *Los Hermanos.*

Despite the encroachment of other cultures, members of the Brotherhood continue to maintain their faith quietly and observe their rituals, including ceremonies which focus on the Passion and death of Jesus Christ. Because of this, oftentimes the Brothers have been greatly misunderstood. Their intimate and often symbolic acts of penance and devotion, carried out in private in their meeting places called moradas, have been sensationalized by many writers and historians. Although the Brotherhood's origins remain shrouded in mystery and its activities have been frequently misconstrued, its importance to the cultural heritage of New Mexico and the Catholic Church can never be denied.

On the historic Santa Fe plaza during that Spanish Market, we came across a young santero who knew full well the importance of the Hermandad to his way of life. The young man was a member in good standing of the Brotherhood. We had met him and other members of his family in their village. It was good to see him again, surrounded by the retablos and bultos he had been carving throughout the winter and spring.

In the midst of his beautifully carved santos covering the table stood a bulto known as *Doña Sebastina*, or *El Ángel de la Muerte*. An important icon that serves as a vivid reminder of mortality and the need to prepare for death, this lone figure was shrouded in black cloth and a veil. Her eyes were costume-jewelry pearls, and in her smiling mouth was a single tooth. The young santero with a round face grinned when he explained to us that the tooth was one of his own. We realized the dark angel was special. We gently lifted her from the table. *La Muerte* had found a home.

By evening, the foot-tall figure of death was in a special place on a shelf in a small apartment in the Barrio de Analaco, the oldest neighborhood in Santa Fe. A branch of cedar and some river stones were placed around her. Nearby was a retablo of San Miguel, the archangel, and some vigil candles, rows of books, and other treasures.

The young Hermano would be pleased. He understood that when he is an old man and has spent his lifetime carving saints and other holy images from cottonwood and aspen, no matter where she resides, the angel of death with pearly eyes and his own baby tooth will still be smiling.

Saturday's Heroes

Inspired by the first silent-picture western characters, this legion of big-screen cowboys and cowgirls and their faithful sidekicks were who every red-blooded American youngster flocked to see at neighborhood movie matinées during the heyday of the western motion picture. Included in the posse of Hollywood heroes and heroines were Roy Rogers and Dale Evans, Gene Autry, Hopalong Cassidy, and many others. Some of them made the transition to television. All of them are memorable.

■

On October 12, 1940, Tom Mix — the

real "king of the cowboys" — made his last ride. It was a Saturday — the day of the week reserved for the movie matinées that Mix had made so popular and which had made him famous.

That morning, invading Nazi troops poured into Bucharest. Brave Londoners cleaned up debris from German bombs that had destroyed whole city blocks but missed the great dome of Saint Paul's Cathedral, which stood battered but erect as a symbol of British resolve. From Rome came headlines of Pope Pius and his denouncement of women for bowing to the "tyranny of fashion." In New York, Mickey Rooney and Judy Garland were breathless after the Broadway opening of *Strike up the Band*. Baseball fans in Cincinnati nursed hangovers after the triumph of their Reds over the Detroit Tigers to take the World Series in seven games.

Tom Mix was far away from the fields of war, sport, and politics. He was in Arizona — ancient home of the Apache, the gunfighter, the cavalry dragoon. He was in the land that he and other early western film stars had helped to make indelible in the minds of moviegoers around the world.

Wearing an immaculate white suit, a ten-gallon hat, and the fanciest tooled boots that money could buy, Mix told friends that he felt as fit as a young bronc rider. Fans who saw him that day when he paused for lunch never guessed that he was in his sixtieth year. He was tanned and trim, and his hair was still as black as the coal mined from the Pennsylvania countryside where he was born.

Mix drove his custom-built Cord — a lemon-yellow automobile with his raised initials on the tread of the tires. Millions of movie fans had adored his trick horse, Tony, but Mix also took pride in knowing that he was the first cowboy star to use the auto in western films.

By twilight, the heavens over the Arizona desert were deep red, the color of enchilada sauce. There was a bite to the air, and from the foothills and the thickets of creosote and yucca came the first evening songs of the coyotes. At a ramshackle filling station, a grease monkey pumped gasoline into the Cord, and warned Mix to be on the lookout because a bridge was out and there were detours near the town of Florence. Mix doffed his big white hat to signal adiós, and pushed on toward the glitter of Hollywood. The Cord roared away, leaving a trail of *TMs* imprinted in the thick dust.

The son of a poor couple with four children to raise, Mix had come far since his birth at Mix Run, Pennsylvania. He dropped out of school after the fourth grade. He spent much of his time prowling the hallowed battleground at Gettysburg and listening to old men who recalled the great westward migration of pioneers in Conestoga wagons, "the ships of the desert," manufactured in nearby Lancaster. From his father, a coachman and superintendent of stables for a wealthy family, Mix gained a love of horseflesh. The boy's imagination was fired by dime novels and visits to Buffalo Bill's Wild West performances, when the flamboyant Cody and his troop of daring riders came to town.

Good looks proved Mix's greatest asset and made him the center of attention when he was a strapping eighteen-year-old in his new army uniform, primed and ready to take on all comers in the Spanish-American War. But he saw no action and grew restless. Yearning for excitement and adventure, he finally took off. Mix left barracks life behind and struck out for the adventure of the Old West he hoped to find in Oklahoma Territory. He was not disappointed.

The young man tended bar, hired on as a cowhand, and even wore the star of a peace officer for a time. Technically, he was an army deserter, but that did not stop him from joining "the Cowboy Brigade" that rode up Pennsylvania Avenue to celebrate Theodore Roosevelt's presidential inauguration in 1905.

Mix's finest early days were spent on the Miller Brothers' 101 Ranch in Oklahoma. He started cowboying there for fifteen dollars a month and board, and within a year, he was made livestock foreman and a rodeo star. In only a matter of time, William Selig, an ingenious moviemaker, and some other early film producers took notice and put Mix to work in their moving pictures. Twenty years later, Mix was earning $17,500 a week, making him the highest-paid Hollywood star of his day.

Reporters would ask him about his life, and he had a pat answer. He would flash his biggest grin and say, "I attribute my present standing to the training I received and experienced when working under the 101 brand. I could name hundreds of incidents and scenes in my pictures that really had their origin along the banks of the old Salt Fork River."

But on that Saturday evening in October 1940, those wild days and nights with the Miller boys on the 101 Ranch must have seemed like lifetimes past. Mix had endured five marriages, earned and lost millions of dollars, made countless trips around the world, and cranked out hundreds of shoot-'em-up movies for his fans. He also had witnessed a total transformation in the motion-picture industry. Although he owned a Hollywood mansion equipped with an English butler and a huge electric sign on the front lawn that displayed his name in lights, Mix yearned for the old days. Sometimes the 101 and the Millers and those dusty rodeo arenas seemed so distant.

Mix tried his damndest not to let the past slip away. Through the years, he made it a point to get together with other old-timers to reminisce about the years of glory on the 101 and bygone times at early Hollywood saloons and gathering places where the term *drugstore cowboy* was coined. But after the talking stopped and they all went their separate ways, the truth sunk in once again. Mix knew deep in his heart that his trail was about played out.

He had earned and lost millions in an attempt to revive his career with yet another Wild West circus tour. The movie roles dried up too. His speaking voice was never that good, and talkies took their toll. The last picture he had made was a serial back in 1935. "Singing cowboys," such as Gene Autry and Roy Rogers were the rage. Still, Mix never gave up. Earlier that year, Mix had paid a visit to his old studio, now 20th Century Fox, to seek out John Ford, a tough Irishman and one of the most respected directors in Hollywood. Ford was busy shooting *The Grapes of Wrath*, but he made time to take the old cowboy star to lunch. They talked about their experiences in the late teens and twenties, when Ford was trying out his director's wings and Mix had built a reputation as the "Lochinvar of the plains." When they finished their club sandwiches and switched from whiskey to coffee, Ford looked Mix in the eye and told him the hard truth. The picture business had passed him by. Ford knew the old cowboy would want it straight, with no sugar coating.

Other old pals at Fox told Mix the same thing. After Ford went back to the set, Mix looked for R. Lee "Lefty" Hough, the studio production manager. They shook hands and bear-hugged, and Mix sat in his office and they talked. Like Ford, Lefty pulled no punches. Then Mix went to the office of Sol Wurtzel, the studio manager.

"I could see he was quite depressed," Wurtzel would say years later. "Finally, I walked with him to the gate. He said, 'Sol, I don't know what I'm going to do.' I couldn't answer. He stood there in the vestibule, and there were pictures of all the big stars, Tyrone Power and everyone else, on the wall. Here was the one guy that had made our goddamn studio what it was, looking for a spot."

But Mix tried not to let those bad experiences pull him down. He knew he had to endure the tough times and come back, as he always had before. Just the day before his trip across the Arizona desert, he had received a much needed boost when he visited some old friends in the Gila country. They were people who knew horses and loved to watch a good chase. They were people who still appreciated Mix as an actor and as a man. They were people who knew the best thing a rider could do when a stallion pitched him off was to climb back on and hold tight.

They told Mix he could do it. They told him he could return to Hollywood and start again. He could take center stage. They told him he would always be the "king of the cowboys." They gave him plenty to think about on his trip back to California.

On the lonely desert road, evening shade approached. Pairs of Inca doves fluttered to the telephone wires stretched alongside the narrow road. Eighteen miles south of Florence on Highway 89, a work crew was about to knock off after a long day repairing a bridge over a dry wash. They just had put up detour signs and wooden barriers when they spied a cloud of dust and saw the Cord speeding along. The lemon-yellow car never slowed down. It crashed through the barrier and flipped over in the wash. Workmen rushed to the scene and dragged Mix clear of the wreckage.

They found him impeccably dressed, unmarked by wounds, and stone-dead. His neck was broken, apparently by a metal suitcase stashed in the car. Hollywood legend soon filled the suitcase with twenty-dollar gold pieces. Mix's life had been ended by the very stuff that, as far as he was concerned, had given it meaning. Sunday-morning newspaper headlines screamed the news, which was met mostly with disbelief.

In Hollywood, Mix's friends and fans gathered to say their farewells. When his estate tried to secure an American flag from the Veterans Administration to cover the casket during the funeral, the question of Mix's having been an army deserter was raised once more. When officials refused to provide a flag, John Ford intervened. He finally called in some chits and a flag was eventually obtained. Mix was buried with full military and Masonic honors. They laid him to rest in the Whispering Pines section of Forest Lawn. He was buried in his best outfit, complete with glossy black boots. His belt buckle spelled out his name in diamonds.

Out in the Arizona desert at the place where the Cord had tumbled off the road, a statue of a riderless pony was erected to mark the spot of Mix's death. At 20th Century Fox, people also remembered. On one of the big soundstages, they placed a bronze plaque dedicated to the memory of Tom Mix and his horse, Tony.

Years after his death, youngsters with hope in their hearts and stardust in their eyes hurried by the stage on their way to an audition. Some of them noticed the plaque. Only a few asked about Mix. Those who did got the same answer. Grizzled stagehands or a director who happened to be nearby set the record straight.

"Who was Tom Mix, you ask. Don't you know, kid? Why, he was hot stuff around here. He was the 'king of the cowboys.' "

Skid Road

In loggers' lingo, the road or path through the woods over which logs were dragged — at first by horses, mule, or oxen, and later by mechanical means. Also, this term was applied to the districts in lumber towns such as Seattle where rowdy saloons provided refuge and relief for carousing crews of loggers. Eventually, *skid road* came to mean squalid neighborhoods frequented by derelicts and winos. It gave rise to the slang misnomer *skid row.*

■

In the midst of the fog-shrouded rain forest of the Olympic Peninsula — part of that dense forest ranging from California to Alaska known by loggers as the big woods — are muted trees choked with club moss and ferns. From this forest primeval surges the Hoh River, a glacier-fed artery rushing from Mount Olympus to the Pacific surf. During what the Indians who lived in this region knew as "the time before everything changed," mammoth stands of timber rose in a solid phalanx along not only the Hoh valley but also Puget Sound and the Strait of San Juan de Fuca. It was old growth — virgin wood — already twelve or fourteen feet across at the butt when the Vikings were on the prowl. Some cedars were seventy feet around.

With the coming of the whites, only ship captains respected the skyscrapers, each conifer representing a potential schooner mast. But to the trappers and settlers called "stump farmers," the monstrous trees were only larger versions of the salmonberry and vine maple that had to be cleared away to plant crops. They cussed the big woods and called them "the green desert."

It took an entire generation and a series of events such as the Chicago fire, the Klondike gold rush, and the San Francisco earthquake to make folks realize the value of "the green desert." The demand for wood has not diminished, but the methods of getting wood to market have changed. In some ways, so have the loggers who are called on to get the job done.

The early logging crews were rough and profane — not a cull in the lot. They were men who lived violent lives in the forest where they were crushed and maimed by logs and machines, and in mill towns where they brawled over card games and whores. They lived in an era when daredevil high climbers rigged spar trees and fallers balanced on springboards, using keen-edged, double-headed axes and two-man saws — "misery whips" — to conquer the timber. Ox and horse teams dragged logs from the woods over skid roads greased with boiled dogfish livers. Steam-powered "donkeys" handled much of the work until the 1920s, when gas and diesel machines took over. Big companies maintained railway networks, moving loggers and machines like chessmen. Logging camps dotted the woods. Men prospered on cookhouse vittles, and jungled up in lice-ridden bunks. There were no hard hats or accident insurance. Reforestation did not exist — it was clear-cut, burn, and run.

Although we firmly believe in efforts to preserve the spotted owl — the creature that requires old-growth forest for habitat and has polarized environmentalists and timber companies — and we deplore logging techniques that have led to wholesale clear-cutting and destruction of irreplaceable stands of ancient timber, we still enjoy the company of loggers.

We hope there is a Valhalla for loggers — a place with sweet water and lots of shade. As the U.S. Marine ballad said, they've served their time in hell. Loggers are proud, and their pride is epidemic. They fit into a single day events that would be high points in anyone else's lifetime. They battle brush, fire, and mud slides, and consider rain a guest that has overstayed its visit. When they get some time off, they don't rest but test their logging skills in heated contests. Loggers know how to build a fire with wet wood and a bit of pitch on a snowy day, and they can roll a cigarette in a hailstorm. They quiver when big timber crashes down a mountain, and they deal with the death and pain that go with the job. They are a special breed.

One of us spent time on the Olympic Peninsula, living in one of the last logging camps and working side by side with loggers, setting choker chains around huge fallen trees. It was incredibly dangerous and difficult work, scrambling over mountainsides with the loggers of the big woods — those loggers known as tramps and those called homeguards.

A homeguard logger has a wife, kids, and monthly payments. A tramp wants no part of that. A tramp goes north when it turns warm, and returns to the lower forty-eight for winter. He is broke when he hits town, broke when he leaves. A tramp carries all he owns on his back. Some tramp loggers are on the run from the law, a woman, or from themselves, and they change their names with every job.

No matter if the man was a tramp or a homeguard, a choker setter or a camp cook, we found that the loggers we were most drawn to were those who labored as tree fallers.

To see the big timber fall usually meant climbing cliffs and hiking narrow paths chiseled in rock. Sometimes the ground is perpendicular, and loggers wrap ropes around their waists and are lowered to the trees. Even seasoned fallers can feel insignificant when sunlight seeps through cathedrals of fir.

We recall an early morning spent watching fallers as they silently made their way, with fifty-pound chain saws balanced like rifles on their shoulders. They were as serene as priests, and they spoke gently to the timber as if it were a woman they had come to rescue.

The Douglas fir they had come to harvest rose 250 feet into the clouds and had lived on the mountain for six hundred years. Eagles had preened in its branches, lightning had scarred its thick hide. It was overripe and loaded with rot. The loggers knew it should have been taken long ago, but they were the first to reach it. They passed a thermos of hot tea and rested. They patted and stroked the tree. There was no hurry.

On high ground, a falling giant can easily shatter, and the cutters wanted to save as much timber as possible. They measured the tree with eye and ax, searching for "widow-makers" — dangling limbs or chunks of bark that might fall on unwary woodmen. They checked the lay of the land. A good faller can drop a tree on a stake if all goes well.

The fallers made an undercut notch in the base of the tree to create a point of weakness and determine the direction it would fall when severed in back. If necessary, wedges and even a hydraulic jack can be used to ensure that a tree falls in the right place. Nobody ever yells "Timber!" and no one with sense calls a big woods logger "lumberjack." That's only in the movies or in other parts of the country. As a veteran faller finished the back cut, he chanted, "Whoa . . . whoa . . . goin' south . . . watch 'er roll . . . whoa." It was a mournful cry that echoed over the forest.

The fir shuddered. Its heart cracked and it moaned, plunging down the mountainside in a furious explosion of bark and earth. The fallers jumped on the bleeding stump and saw that they were on the mark — the big fir was saved. It would provide enough lumber to build several new homes.

A light rain became sleet and then turned to rain again. More loggers moved in with chain saws to slice up the fir. The rain slowed, and a rainbow appeared over the valley.

In the evening, when we were finished with work and had returned to camp for a big supper that included T-bone steaks piled six high wheat-cake style, we went to town to drink icy beer and nurse our wounds.

We paused not far from the lusty town of Forks, Washington, to pay our respects to a cedar known as the world's largest. It was a western red cedar, *Thuga plicata*, standing 178 feet high and more than nineteen feet in diameter. It was probably two thousand years old, and completely surrounded by clear-cut. Some miles away, nearer the coast, we knew of another cedar, maybe even larger, also in a clear-cut. People tattooed the cedars with their initials and sayings such as, "Woodman, spare this tree." Both trees were gnarled and varicose. It was like visiting old war veterans, toothless and deaf, worth seeing because they were the last ones.

Every once in a while, we think about those old trees and wonder if they are still standing. We pray that they are, but just to be safe, we vow never to return.

To me a tramp logger is a true independent —a man who won't eat shit for a job. If somebody doesn't treat him right, a tramp doesn't snivel or hang his head about it — he's down the road, partner, and gone. Being a tramp is a pride thing more than anything else. I'd rather die a busted-up old man in some sleazy hotel — die all alone — than wind up being a cull who can't get out of bed and go to the mirror and look himself in the face.

— Robert Fudge, tramp logger

Sky City

A name for Acoma, New Mexico, a Native American pueblo established ca. 1075 in present northwestern New Mexico. Also the name of the tribe, "people of the white rock."

▪

The most spectacular of all pueblo communities, Acoma is often called the oldest continuously inhabited city in the United States, despite the same claim by people living in the ancient Hopi village of Oraibi, in neighboring Arizona. Whether it's the oldest or not, the fact remains that the Sky City of Acoma was built on a seventy-acre sandstone mesa jutting 367 feet above the desert floor centuries before Spanish conquistadores stumbled on the settlement while searching for the fabled Seven Cities of Cibola.

Originally, the pueblo was reached only by using ladder steps and toeholds and fingerholds cut in the face of the steep rock. A formidable refuge for Indians fleeing Spanish invaders, Acoma has successfully resisted change despite the intrusion of Catholic priests and missionaries and, in recent times, a steady flow of visitors traveling on U.S. 66 and Interstate 40, a dozen miles to the north. A road now leads to Sky City, but the pueblo, where only fifty Acomans live year-round, remains unapproachable unless visitors, many seeking the coveted Acoma pottery, obtain official permits and passes and abide by pueblo etiquette.

Still, we believe the best way to visit Acoma is not to go there at all. Just look at it from afar, sitting on the mesa up in the clouds. Sometimes we do that; we drive near Acoma, but we don't stop until we are farther down the road. We might not stop until we get to McCarty's, a trading community on Acoma land. We like to visit the mission church there that was built by Indians, and look at the hand-carved beams and religious figures. Indians who worship there often leave a turquoise nugget or a sacred feather instead of lighting a candle. We have seen baskets of bread placed on the altar. One winter morning, we climbed the steep slope behind the church and found fresh mountain-lion tracks in the new snow. Then we sat down on the rocks with the wind in our faces and, without even seeing the old pueblo, we imagined how Acoma was in the faraway past and how it will be in the distant future.

Smokey Bear

Probably the world's most famous bear, Smokey Bear (never Smokey *the* Bear) is best known as the U.S. Forest Service's living symbol of national fire prevention.

▪

We are saddened whenever a bear leaves its mountain refuge and comes to town. In parts of the West, drought, fire, or other whims of nature sometimes force bears to lumber into civilization in search of a meal or a drink of cool water.

Under the cover of darkness while neighborhood watchdogs bark their challenge, the bears silently pad down alleys and streets, sniffing through garbage cans. By dawn's early light, some bears, confronted by milk trucks and joggers, panic and make their escape by shinnying up the closest tree. Too often, when the city yawns awake, delinquent bears can be seen hanging onto the tops of elms shading the streets.

In the best-case scenario, some kind people show up with nets and tranquilizer guns. The marooned bear is removed safely and returned to its natural habitat.

But sometimes nothing goes right, and the bear ends up injured or dead.

Even bears who do not come to town are often put at risk, like the black bears of Yosemite and the big grizzlies of Yellowstone and other national parks. These animals remain in familiar surroundings, but they face other perils. They have to put up with hordes of two-legged invaders who insist on feeding them, and whose campsites make tempting pickings for a curious bear which has lost all fear of humans.

We have often wondered if the tourists guilty of dispensing leftover tuna sandwiches and chocolate-chip cookies to obliging roadside bears operate under the erroneous impression that the large flesh eaters are as benign as cuddly teddy bears. Undoubtedly, some of these same people are also careless with campfires and cigarettes, reckless behavior that can result in devastation. Too bad they fail to use common sense and abide by the words, "Remember, only you can prevent forest fires," familiar advice offered by Smokey Bear, a national icon and true hero.

Few folks know that Smokey was born of necessity. The idea of an amiable bear to educate the American public about fires — mostly started by humans — that annually destroyed millions of acres of forest and rangeland developed in 1942. That was when a Japanese submarine patrolling off the California coast attacked an oil refinery, causing little damage but creating a sense of urgency when some shells exploded near Los Padres National Forest. Fears that future enemy attacks could ignite forest fires, coupled with concern for the nation's lumber supply, propelled the Wartime Advertising Council to answer the U.S. Forest Service's patriotic plea for help and launch a national safety campaign.

It was decided to use the cartoon image

of a bear as a symbol and as a spokesanimal to convey the important safety message. Named for a famous New York City firefighter, "Smokey Joe" Martin, the first rendition of Smokey Bear appeared in public on August 2, 1944, in a Forest Service poster. Drawn by well-known illustrator Albert Staehle, who followed all instructions by giving Smokey an intelligent look and slightly quizzical expression, the bear wore a traditional forest ranger's hat and a pair of blue jeans.

By 1946, another illustrator, Rudy Wendelin, was asked to soften Smokey's looks and give him a friendlier, less stern appearance. The Kansas-born artist did just that. He became Smokey's caretaker until 1973, when he officially retired, although he continued to create new Smokey calendars and posters for many more years.

The fire-prevention campaign acquired a living symbol in 1950 — an orphaned two-month-old, four-pound black bear cub. The young bear was rescued by a firefighting crew not far from the village of Capitán, New Mexico, after a carelessly discarded cigarette butt ignited a blaze in Lincoln National Forest that ultimately destroyed seventeen thousand acres. Badly burned on the buttocks and paws, the valiant little survivor first was given the nickname Hotfoot Teddy. The moniker soon was changed to Smokey Bear after the singed cub recovered and was moved to a permanent home at the National Zoological Park in Washington, D.C.

Eventually, Smokey was allotted his own ZIP code and even had a secretary to answer the millions of fan letters that poured into the zoo. He continued to stand as the embodiment of conservation even after 1975, when this unusual but official employee of the National Park Service retired from public life. Smokey died peacefully in 1976. His body was flown back to New Mexico and laid to rest at Smokey Bear State Historical Park near Capitán, in the shadows of the rugged mountains where it all began.

Songdog

The name given to the coyote by some Native American people.

▪

Coyotes are special creatures — at least, we think so. Coyotes have always been there for us — whether they are creeping like burglars through the ravines of L.A. and the streets of Phoenix, or slipping up on a remote desert camp just to check out our suppertime fire before bursting into song.

Despite being one of the most cherished symbols of the American West, coyotes have been constantly stalked and killed by hunters, trappers, and ranchers who contend that the creature's very existence threatens livestock. We have found that most of the time, the bad rap that folks try to pin on coyotes is an exaggeration or a lie. The animals often are maligned for crimes and misdemeanors they did not commit.

The coyote's name has become a term used by Hispanics to describe the offspring of a mixed marriage, or a half-breed — someone who does not quite belong to either world. And in the chic cities of the Southwest, especially Santa Fe, one tasteless incarnation of the wily animal is the image of a howling coyote used as a model of commercial exploitation by restaurants and curio shops that cater to tourists.

We consider coyotes — known as pranksters, helpers, seducers, fools, and friends — some of our best teachers. The coyote name we like to use is one that comes from Native Americans. They called the coyote God's dog, or sometimes songdog, because they believe the coyote sang the world into existence. That is the name that fits the best — songdog.

Resilient and elusive, songdogs refuse to disappear. Those methodical attempts at extermination have only made them more resourceful. They adapt and survive. They are defiant in every sense of the word. The songdog's range has even spread to places where they were previously unknown. And right along with the animals themselves, the myth of the songdog continues to grow. Contemporary Native American stories about the songdog flourish. Songdogs live on in various forms and styles across the land.

Another type of songdog exists besides the animal coyote, *Canis latrans*. The revered and reviled four-legged icon serves as a metaphor, helping to illustrate the coyote's characteristics and peculiarities that occur in other forms, such as in the two-legged variety of songdog.

In truth, every person has at least a little bit of songdog. Everyone has a story to tell, a song to sing. Just listen for the songdog and open up your mind.

> *Coyotes live it up*
> *till morning.*
> *They don't even*
> *care what day it is.*
>
> — William Stafford
> *"Oregon Haiku"*

Tequila

An alcoholic beverage that is steeped in history and obscured by fables. Tequila comes from the maguey, or, agave plant, specifically the agave tequilana, also known as agave azul, or blue agave. Other alcoholic beverages come from the agave, such as pulque, fermented agave sap and the oldest drink in North America, and mezcal, a potent, clear liquor. Tequila is a type of mezcal, but unlike its cousins — pulque and mezcal — tequila must be made only from the blue agave.

■

A long, long time ago, when the Toltecs still ruled Mexico, there was a deity named Quetzalcóatl, the Plumed Serpent. He was the god of the wind and patron of the arts and culture. He was unlike anyone ever seen in Mexico, with his light skin, blue eyes, and beard. There was a human Quetzalcóatl as well — a Toltec king who, as high priest of this deity, was called by his name. But a rival ruler, jealous of Quetzalcóatl's power, got him drunk on five cups of pulque, the ferment of the agave plant and an ancestor to tequila. Quetzalcóatl was so embarrassed by his drunkenness that he went to the sea, built a raft of snakeskins, and sailed into exile, vowing to return in the year of "One Reed." As the fates would have it, that turned out to be 1519, the year Hernán Cortés and his conquistadores splashed ashore. The Aztecs, who were in power then, mistook Cortés, fair-skinned and bearded, for the exiled god-king. The rest, as they say, is history. But to this day, in parts of Mexico, some Indians still patiently wait for the return of their ruler, the essence of life on earth. And there are still others who firmly believe that Quetzalcóatl walks among them.

▪

We both thought that the taxi had the look of a prizefighter who had lost one too many bouts. The fenders and chrome were battered, but a covey of plastic saints residing on the dashboard did its duty, and the cab emerged unscathed from the snarls of traffic. It scooted down the streets and boulevards of Guadalajara to the front door of the Bar Cue.

The ancient saloon squatting in the shadows looked its age. On the sidewalk out front, children peddled figs and peaches. Across the street in a small plaza, old shoeshine men sat by their wooden stands, waiting for twilight.

Inside the cantina, a waiter twice our age waved us to a table and asked our pleasure. He shuffled off to fetch bottles of *aqua mineral* as we looked over the yellowing bullfight posters on the walls, and the knots of men who sat around us, working on their glasses of courage.

"Salud!" A well-lubricated patron standing at the long bar downed a shot of tequila macho style — a lick of salt from the back of his hand, a stream of tequila down his throat, and a squeeze of lime on his tongue. He wiped his sleeve across his mouth and smacked his lips in tribute.

"That fellow has no taste," said a nearby voice. We turned to see a Mexican man sitting alone at another table. He nodded to us and told the waiter to bring "the usual — the very best tequila you possess." The request was delivered quickly to the barman, who went to an array of tequila bottles and reached without hesitation for the one with a blue horseshoe on the label. It was Tequila Herradura, a most mellow drink from a small but prestigious distillery that had been making fine tequila since 1870.

The stranger lifted his brimming *copita,* and we could see a smile appear beneath his manicured mustache and beard. He studied the golden tequila that had been aged in hand-hewed oak barrels, sniffed the glass, and then sipped gently. "You never gulp tequila," the stranger told the waiter and anyone else within earshot, including us. "Savor tequila as you would an exquisite painting or a fine wine or a lovely woman. There is an art to drinking tequila." He winked his *saluds* at the waiter and then at us, and sipped again. "This is truly magnificent tequila."

We sat back and enjoyed the scene. It was a splendid moment, just being there in a quiet bar watching the stranger enjoy the best tequila in the world.

Whenever we think of Mexico, certain images come to mind — bullfights, sunsets the color of enchiladas, Pancho Villa and, always, tequila. For so long, people have quenched their thirsts with it. Each year, tens of millions of gallons of tequila are distilled for imbibers in the United States, Canada, Japan, Europe and, of course, Mexico.

No other spirit is as clouded by mystery and myth. This drink that is fit for gods or outlaws is highly appreciated but greatly misunderstood. More lies have been told about tequila than about Billy the Kid, Bigfoot, and George Custer. After years of chasing tequila fables, we realized that finding the truth about tequila is as difficult as catching lightning bugs in a mason jar. Tequila is awash in exaggerations and tales that leave most serious drinkers scratching their heads.

"*¿Señor y Señora?*" We snapped out of our thoughts at the sound of the stranger's voice. "Come join me, *por favor*," he asked with a wide smile and a broad gesture of his head to two chairs at his table. We smiled back and went to the stranger's table. He grabbed the waiter and ordered a round of tequilas backed up by sangrita, a chaser made from citrus and tomato juices, chili sauce, and salt. "*Salud!*" he said again while taking yet another long sip from his glass.

"There is no mystery to tequila," the man told us. "The problem is, so much of the tequila today is like a cheap whore. The industry has dropped its standards, and they are putting sugar, colorings, water, and only God knows what else into what is supposed to be pure tequila. In truth, only the juices of one plant, and one plant alone — the blue agave — should ever be used for tequila. Nothing more!"

We asked the stranger how to tell if you are being served good tequila. "Ah, my friends, you will know at once. Tequila is a kind of drink that when it is good, it is really good, but when it is bad. . . ." The man's voice trailed off, and he frowned. Then he snapped his fingers, and the waiter brought another serving of tequilas and a plate of freshly sliced mangoes for us to nibble on between sips.

"To truly know tequila, to understand tequila," the stranger continued, "you need to remember some important facts. Remember that three alcoholic beverages — pulque, mezcal, tequila — come from a plant called the agave, or the maguey. Agaves are in the amaryllis family, and they are not — definitely not — related to cacti." The man's frown returned at the mere idea.

"Pulque is just a fermented drink, but tequila and mezcal are distilled, although mezcal is distilled only once and it can be made from different kinds of agaves. To be authentic, tequila must come only from the blue agave which flourishes in the rich volcanic soil of the Mexican state of Jalisco. Tequila is distilled twice and must be bottled on estate with absolutely no additives. Tequila is the best type of mezcal, just as cognac is the best kind of brandy."

The man paused again, and we all lifted our glasses in unison. The tequila went down like velvet. The flavor lingered. After a moment, the man continued his lecture.

"Tequila gets its name from a small town in Jalisco, about forty miles northwest of us here in Guadalajara. That is where the blue agave likes to grow. Oh, yes, please do remember this also — there are no worms in bottles of tequila. You only find worms in bottles of mezcal."

More long sips trickled down our throats. With only a glance, the stranger signaled the waiter to fetch more plates of limes and mangoes and replenish our stock of sangrita.

"And there is something else that bothers me," continued the stranger. "That drink you call the margarita is purely a creation of the United States. It is not in a Mexican's nature to drink tequila that way. And no matter what you hear about fancy bartenders in Los Angeles or San Antonio inventing the drink, you need to know that a fellow in Juárez named Pancho Morales made the first margarita. It was on July 4, 1942. Morales lived in El Paso and drove a milk truck for a living. I understand he preferred to drink scotch." The stranger's laughter echoed throughout the bar.

What about pulque, we asked the man. "It is 'heaven's water,' " he told us. He sighed and fell silent for a moment. "Tequila and mezcal were conjured up by the Spanish when their brandy and rum supplies ran out. But when they arrived here, they found the Aztecs drinking pulque. It is the oldest alcoholic beverage in North America, and about as powerful as beer. It tastes like sour milk to some, rotten apples and gunpowder to others, and one man once said it was like drinking wallpaper paste laced with mucilage. The Toltecs came up with pulque in the tenth century, but I know how it was really invented. It all started with a mouse."

Again the man's laughter thundered across the cantina.

"It was during the reign of Tepancaltzin, eighth ruler of the Toltecs," he said. "A nobleman spied a mouse chewing a hole in the base of an agave plant. The man tasted the curdy juice that oozed out, and he liked it. To make points with the king, the man sent his daughter, Xochitl, with a bowl of the juice to the palace. Apparently the king was more impressed by the damsel than the brew. The pair of them hit it off, and from their union came a child named Meconetzin, or Child of the Maguey."

We wondered about the legend that says pulque led to the Toltecs' downfall and the exile of Quetzalcóatl. The stranger told us that it was all true. His smile left, and he stared at the table, cluttered with glasses and empty plates. We summoned the waiter and ordered three more tequilas.

"Pulque was sacred to the Aztecs," said the man, revived by the fresh drink. "They used it as an offering to their gods, especially the god of fire. They placed the drink in vessels in front of a fire or sprinkled it around the hearth to honor the gods."

He went on to tell us how the Aztecs carried on a love-hate relationship with pulque. They thought of it as a sacred substance and a social evil. They tried to restrict its use for warriors, nursing mothers, the elderly, and condemned prisoners. Excessive drinking was controlled by a ban on the "fifth cup," in memory of Quetzalcóatl's drinking binge.

"In Aztec mythology, there was a pulquería in one corner of the night sky where the gods gathered and drank," said the stranger. "The heavenly tavern had four hundred udders, one for each of the pulque gods, and it was operated by Marahuel, the goddess of pulque."

The man's blue eyes sparkled, but he seemed to be far away. Together, we lifted our *copitas* of tequila once more and licked up the last drops. Then the stranger stood, bowed to us and then to the waiter, and turned to leave the bar. I asked him to stay for just one more round.

"No, *señor*, no more for me, *gracias*. I have had four, and that is my limit. *Adiós*."

He walked out of the Bar Cue into the street, where twilight had given way to darkness.

"You owe me nothing," said the waiter while he picked up the empty glasses and left us two more tequilas.

"Who was that man?" we asked.

"I do not know, my friends. He comes in sometimes and he drinks alone. He sits at this table and has his four tequilas and then he leaves."

We took our nightcaps and stood in the doorway, and saw that a summer rain had passed. It left the air clean and ripe, but there still was a trace of the smell of ripe fruit and shoe polish. It was a star-studded tequila evening in Jalisco that could make even Quetzalcóatl come home. We splashed the rest of our drinks on the floor to salute the old gods, and stalked off to find a taxi.

Tumbleweed

Popular name for several bushy plants, such as Russian thistle, found throughout most parts of the West; also called rolling bush, white man's plant, prickly glasswort, Russian cactus, saltwort, and wind witch.

▪

When tumbleweeds stop growing, late in the year, they break off close to the ground. The wind rolls them across highways and prairies, and they pile up against barbed-wire fences or fill arroyos and ditches. A few of them just keep going.

Accidentally introduced to the western United States in the 1870s, tumbleweeds generally are considered nuisances by farmers and may be dangerous to motorists who encounter them. We once saw one as big as a Volkswagen plodding along in eastern New Mexico, and we were afraid the thing would devour us and our car.

Popularized by western movies, this immigrant weed shares a particular kinship with the fiddle-footed person, or vagabond. The tumbleweed is by far the best traveler on the high plains, a symbol of footloose western rovers, people with gypsy hearts who are likely to drift in any direction and not stay in any one place too long.

Because tumbleweeds spend a lot more time in the wind than in the ground, they are not much use for cover, shade, or holding the soil in place. On the plains, from the point of view of humans, the tumbleweed's main function is poetic. They roll and bounce on the wind, they fly through the air like half-filled weather balloons, they pile up in throngs against fences and buildings. The poet Anselm Hollo has written that a tumbleweed "looks like the skeleton of a brain."

— Ian Frazier
Great Plains

U.S. Route 66

The most famous highway in the United States, possibly in the world, this path of concrete and asphalt between Chicago, Illinois, and Santa Monica, California, was christened in 1926. It traverses eight states, three time zones, and more than twenty-four hundred miles. Although Route 66 travelers may journey east or west, most people view the highway as a westward path known by other names, including the Main Street of America and the Mother Road.

▪

When we are out on Route 66, we are at home. For us, the highway is a long village that stretches from the shores of Lake Michigan all the way to the Pacific surf. We know many of the old haunts and secret places along the road's path — the diners,

greasy spoons, tourist traps, motor courts, garages, and trading posts, as well as the natural attractions. More importantly, we are honored to call friends many of the people who live and work on the shoulders of the Mother Road.

Hundreds of personal stories from our Route 66 adventures and travels keep us company. They are not very complicated episodes of our lives, just special moments to cherish always. Many are sweet, a few are sad and even bitter. Some are pure magic.

One of those magical moments came while we were traveling east on Route 66 with a Texas friend. We had chased the old year away at Gallup. On New Year's Day 1989, we found ourselves on a battered Route 66 railroad bridge in high New Mexican desert country between Acoma and Albuquerque, just past Laguna Pueblo.

We pulled the car to the side of the highway, all varicose and scarred, and walked to the center of the rickety bridge. Below us the Atchison, Topeka, and Santa Fe railroad tracks — ribbons of gleaming steel — ran in either direction as far as we could see.

Twilight crept across the land, and the mountains and desert turned rosy. It seemed to be warmer, even though the air was frosty and would turn even colder when the sun finally vanished for the night. We stood there watching the traffic on the distant interstate highway. The trucks moved slowly up a slight incline. They looked like big white slugs creeping along under great clouds the color of ripe peaches. Pairs of ravens, black as shiny coal, danced like marionettes on the telegraph wires next to the tracks. Way off in the distance, we heard a train moan.

Finally we saw the engine and the long line of freight cars approaching from the east. The three of us lay down on the bridge. We stretched out side by side and waited. The train moaned some more as it drew closer and closer to the bridge. We could make out the big yellow and blue engine, and we raised up and waved at the engineer and crew. They answered with another salute of the horn that carried across the sagebrush to our perch.

The train finally reached the bridge and, as it shot below, a wave of hot air rushed over us as we lay on the road above. We felt the bridge and the scarred asphalt tremble. Just as the engine was emerging from beneath the bridge, the engineer, with a pipe clenched in his teeth and the last rays of the sun glinting off his eyeglasses, blew the diesel horn once again. At that precise moment, as the warmth of that train washed across the cracked pavement and us, the Mother Road came to life. All of it was resurrected — the path of the dust bowlers and migrants, the road of soldiers going off to war, the highway of vacationers and travelers, the artery for dreamers and seekers of magic.

We jumped to our feet and ran to the other side of the bridge. We saw the long train racing westward, down the ribbons of steel, into the approaching night. We watched until the train was long gone and out of sight. Then we returned to the car and left the bridge. No one spoke a word until we were many miles away, close to the lights of the city.

Viva Las Vegas

Literally, "Long live Las Vegas." Also, the name of a song and an Elvis Presley film from 1964.

▪

It used to be that when we were roaming the West and wanted to do some major-league people watching, we could always slip into Las Vegas. That Gomorrah on the desert was just the place to turn over some rocks and see who or what crawled out.

Every size, shape, and persuasion of humanity seemed to find its way to the city that was built on legalized gambling. They turned out in droves to parade up and down the glittering Strip, crowd the nightclubs and wedding chapels, and flock to casinos packed with gaming tables and row after row of gleaming slot machines. We saw them all—winners and losers in polyester, flamboyant high rollers, easy marks and wide-eyed rubes, GIs with fresh haircuts and loads of testosterone, Damon Runyon thugs, leggy showgirls, sunbaked desert rats, and sad gambling addicts bound to wheelchairs, feeding their life savings to the slots.

Times have changed, and so has Vegas.

This city that grew by leaps and bounds—thanks to sin and easy divorce—has been transformed into what has been called a "desert Disneyland," complete with theme parks and colossal hotels catering to families and convention trade. It is no longer "adults only," but a sort of wacky all-American city where kids can play video games while parents try their luck at blackjack.

The movers and shakers figured out that to guarantee their city's future existence, it was necessary for Las Vegas to clean up at least part of its sometimes outrageous act. As a result, "the mirage that grew out of Bugsy Siegel's mid-century vision of showgirls and slot machines" — as the *New York Times* once put it — has evolved into a huge metropolitan area of riotous high-tech architecture, suburban housing developments, and water parks that reflects the values of the rest of the country. There will always be acres of crap tables and slots, but the old mobster image that put Vegas on the map has been replaced by wholesome entertainment aimed at mainstream Americans. The sleazy strippers and foulmouthed comics have given way to magicians and figure skaters. Vegas has become a destination for PTA presidents, retirees, and Boy Scouts.

We have to look elsewhere when we want to people watch. There are still plenty of authentic characters left lurking in the neon shadows of Las Vegas, but they are endangered species in this city that is devoid of any sentiment. Vegas is in the family way. We might as well go to the mall. Howard Hughes, Bugsy, Liberace, and Elvis must be spinning in their graves.

The Rat Pack would have checked out quickly. There are no showgirls. There are no Runyonesque souls, even if there are people with glazed eyes playing five slot machines at a time with both hands. What one notices now is the children, roaming the casinos and pumping quarters in video arcades as nimbly as their quite average-looking parents.

—Stephen Drucker
The New York Times
February 13, 1994

Wild, Wild West

That great expanse of land that stretches from the Mississippi River to the Pacific coast, from Canada to Mexico.

■

When we hear the cliché "Wild West," we shudder. Hollywood's romanticized images of "noble savages," spirited calvary charges, trailblazing pioneers, and grizzled gunfighters do not come to mind. Instead, our thoughts turn to the vast expanse of uncultivated and unsettled land — great forests, prairies, plains, deserts, and mountains — spreading across the continent from the mighty Mississippi to the Pacific shore. We think of what once was, what is now, and what could be.

We especially are reminded of — and thankful for — three wilderness evangelists from different times and different places who, whether they would have liked it or not, we consider to be spiritual allies in the quest to save the real wild West. But then, Edward Abbey himself put it best when he wrote: "Us nature mystics got to stick together."

▪

John Muir, 1838–1914. Explorer, naturalist, conservationist, author, father of the national park system and founder of the Sierra Club, in 1892.

Major works: Journals, more than three hundred articles and essays, and ten books, including *The Mountains of California*, *Our National Parks*, and *The Yosemite*.

From the beginning, John Muir loved the land. After a two-and-a-half-year stint studying chemistry and geology at the University of Wisconsin, he set out to explore the country. With journal in hand, he hiked from the Ohio River a thousand miles to the Gulf of Mexico before heading west to California. There, the ardent conservationist became known as the premier naturalist and explorer of the High Sierras. Driven by the belief that "only by going alone in silence, without baggage, can one truly get into the heart of the wilderness," Muir and his writings about the Sierra Nevada, Yosemite, and national parks influenced Congress, presidents, and other power brokers to set aside wilderness areas in the West.

In God's wildness lies the hope of the world — the great fresh unblighted, unredeemed wilderness.

— John Muir

▪

Aldo Leopold, 1886–1948. Forest ranger, wildlife ecologist, sport hunter, game manager, artist, essayist, preservationist. Helped found the Wilderness Society, in 1935.

Major works: Journals, essays, newsletters, and the book *A Sand County Almanac and Sketches Here and There.*

We find it fitting that Aldo Leopold, a naturalist and forester who wrote "I love all trees," was the son of a successful furniture manufacturer. It is also fitting that Leopold died while fighting a grass fire. In those last moments, this lover of nature — who had learned about the harmony of nature in a split second while looking into "the fierce green fire" in the eye of a dying wolf — realized his own end was near. He lay down, folded his arms across his chest, and breathed his last. He died with dignity, surrounded by the great outdoors he had championed all his life.

Leopold wrote that the land is abused because "we regard it as a commodity belonging to us." Throughout his life, he remained an eloquent and passionate proponent of the need for a "land ethic." This message came across loud and clear in his prophetic book, *A Sand County Almanac* (heralded by Wallace Stegner as "the utterance of an American Isaiah.") and in all the other work he accomplished, which ultimately led to the landmark Wilderness Act of 1964.

It is a matter of what a man thinks about while chopping, or while deciding what to chop. A conservationist is one who is humbly aware that with each stroke he is writing his signature on the face of his land.

— Leopold Aldo

▪

Edward Abbey, 1927–1989. Novelist, essayist, poet, environmentalist, park ranger.

Major fiction: *The Brave Cowboy, Fire on the Mountain, The Monkey Wrench Gang, The Fool's Progress.*

Major nonfiction: *Desert Solitaire, Slickrock, Cactus Country, Abbey's Road.*

Here is a fellow who liked to say, "Earth. Love it or leave it." Although dubbed "the Thoreau of the American West" by Larry

McMurtry (another of our icons), the Abbey we knew was more like Geronimo or Billy the Kid. Always politically incorrect, Abbey would have hated such comparisons, just as he would have taken serious issue with being included in a listing along with Muir and Leopold. Abbey was pure iconoclast — one hundred proof.

An unadulterated renegade in every sense of the word, this irreverent writer and radical environmentalist whose dream was to see "the whole American West made into a wilderness" produced a steady stream of honest writing — including nineteen fiction and nonfiction books — for a phenomenally loyal audience.

I come more and more to the conclusion that wilderness, in America or anywhere else, is the only thing left that is worth saving.

— Edward Abbey

XIT

One of the best known cattle brands ever, this mark was used by one of the most famous Texas cattle ranches. Founded in 1885 by the Capitol Syndicate, a Chicago corporation, the XIT Ranch once included more than 3,050,000 acres sprawling over ten counties.

▪

Among shelves of books, piles of manuscripts, and stacks of photographs, our study is filled with treasures intended to keep us from harm's way while we do battle with the written word.

On one beam is lashed D.H. Lawrence's double-headed ax, used by the famed English novelist to chop wood during his time in New Mexico. A buffalo skull from the herd at Woolaroc, oil tycoon Frank Phillips' ranch retreat in the Osage Hills of Oklahoma, commands a prominent spot on another beam.

There are other totems — the death mask of "Pretty Boy" Floyd, a Phillips 66 sign replete with bullet holes, rusty spurs, strands of barbed wire, a jug of genuine moonshine, eagle feathers, a hangman's noose from Fort Smith, branding irons, a lucky coyote's fang, old boots, a Route 66 shield, photographs of the famous and infamous, and many other personal mementos.

On top of an antique schoolmarm's desk rest a few nuggets of original Mother Road pavement, a piece of the Berlin Wall, and one of our most prized possessions — a discarded remnant of granite from the Texas capitol, acquired years back during one of the renovations of that venerable edifice in downtown Austin. Few people who pick up the fist-sized chunk of red Texas granite and inspect it ever realize that this piece of Lone Star State history has direct ties to what once was the largest cattle ranch in the world under fence — the XIT.

The story of the birth of the XIT begins in the bad old days when Texas was still trying to bounce back from the Civil War and Reconstruction. Government leaders were weary of their cramped capitol quarters and decided to erect a new building, of imposing size worthy of a state as huge as Texas. The need for a new government palace accelerated in 1881 after a fire destroyed the capitol. The governor quickly summoned lawmakers for a special legislative session, and soon they came up with a plan to get their capitol built.

Although cash poor, the legislators knew they had one significant asset besides a spirited populace — tens of millions of acres that had been deeded by the federal government in 1845 when Texas became part of the United States. By 1882, the legislators put out the word that they would accept bids from any party who wanted to build a new capitol in exchange for three million acres of public lands. It was a true Texas-size job, and hence only two entities submitted bids. One was from a French firm, but it backed out after determining that the task was too monumental. That left only a bid from a group of Chicago financiers headed by brothers Charles and John Farwell.

A deal was struck. In payment for building a $3 million capitol, the midwestern businessmen accepted more than three million acres of rangeland along the New Mexico-Texas border, a spread that easily could have held the entire state of Connecticut.

Everyone was happy. By 1888, Texans had their sparkling new capitol, built with the help of convict labor to cut costs. At the time, it was said to be the fifth-largest building in the world, and the biggest capitol in the nation, with a thirty-story dome — topped by the Goddess of Liberty — a full seven feet higher than the U.S. capitol.

In trade for financing the construction, the syndicate got its land and created the XIT Ranch. Legend has it that the big spread's name and brand of XIT stood for the Roman numeral *X*, or ten, with the first letters of the words *in Texas*, meaning "ten in Texas," since the ranch supposedly took in parts of ten counties.

But old-timers we have encountered out in Dalhart and Dumas and throughout the Panhandle country have a different theory. They point out that in truth, the XIT brand was picked because it was a tough one for rustlers to alter.

No matter how the XIT got its name, it is clear that the ranch was plenty big. Its first windmill was built in 1886. By 1900, 335 windmills were operating on the ranch, which reached from near what is now Lubbock northward to the Oklahoma Panhandle. At one time, more than 150,000 cattle ran over the XIT's ninety-four fenced pastures that required six thousand miles of single-strand barbed wire.

The XIT is long gone. In 1901, the Chicagoans started to sell off small parcels of the ranch at $2.50 per acre. By 1912, they had sold the last of their long-horns. Nowadays, cotton and sunflowers grow where the great XIT cattle herds once grazed.

There is an XIT Museum, with all sorts of displays and exhibits, in Dalhart, and a good book or two that tells all about the history of the ranch. But maybe the most fitting tribute to the old XIT stands tall and proud hundreds of miles away. It is down in Austin — that red granite capitol — still the biggest and best.

. . . prettiest country I ever saw . . . prairie lakes scattered all over it . . . there wasn't a house

or chicken in the whole country. And mirages! You could see anything in the world — just ahead of you.

— Will Rogers
Quoted in *Texas Highways*
June 1991

Yellow Hand

Popular, albeit questionable, name ascribed to a Cheyenne warrior and chief who reportedly was killed and scalped by William Frederick "Buffalo Bill" Cody. The incident was supposed to have occurred on July 17, 1876, in a skirmish at War Bonnet Creek, sometimes called Hat Creek, in northwestern Nebraska. It was just three weeks after the demise of George Custer and elements of the Seventh U.S. Cavalry at Greasy Grass River, also known as the Little Bighorn, in south-central Montana.

▪

Although diehard Wild West fans — the kind who revere Duke Wayne, genuflect before the Alamo, and confuse Hollywood with history — consider it sacrilege, we regard the fabled showman William F. Cody, a.k.a. Buffalo Bill, not just as a legend in his own time but also as a legend in his own mind.

More than anyone else we know of, Cody — an extraordinary figure prone to exaggeration — romanticized and popularized the American West, during his stint as a frontiersman and his even longer career as an entertainer and the subject of hundreds of dime novels. Adroit at riding, shooting, scouting and, of course, slaughtering enormous numbers of buffalo, Cody was the quintessential westerner. His chief attribute was his uncanny ability to attract the limelight to himself.

Idolized by a worldwide audience, including many people in Europe, where by 1890 portraits and statues of Buffalo Bill graced thousands of homes, Cody — with his trademark mustache and goatee and flashy cavalier dress — remained a hero to generations of young Americans. He also had his share of detractors and often was denounced as a womanizer, drunk, charlatan and, above all else, an opportunist. Out of all the endless books, articles, and

films that chronicle, ad nauseam, Cody's factional and fictional exploits, the single episode of his life that we feel is the most telling is the story of his purported scalping of a Cheyenne warrior.

There are, naturally, various versions of this dubious tale, but almost all of them suggest that Cody was so stunned by Custer's demise that he was inspired to seek revenge. The lone Cheyenne whom Cody encountered while snooping around with other cavalry scouts near War Bonnet Creek was the perfect target for avenging the death of Cody's pal.

Fancying himself a bold and noble knight-errant astride a powerful white steed, Cody reportedly fired his Winchester carbine at the warrior, striking him in the leg and killing the pony he was riding. At that exact moment, Cody's horse tripped in a prairie-dog hole, throwing the scout to the ground, where he quickly recovered, took aim, and fired again. The second bullet struck the Cheyenne in the face, killing him instantly. Cody then rushed forward and scalped the slain warrior with a trusty bowie knife.

Cody later recalled, in frequent retellings of the story, that after he lifted the dead man's hair, he held the gruesome trophy aloft and cried out, "The first scalp for Custer!" Then, legend has it, Cody scooped up the Cheyenne's warbonnet, shield, bridle, gun, scabbard, and other personal belongings, and sent them — along with the bloody patch of flesh and hair — to his wife, Louisa. The poor woman reportedly swooned when she tore open the package and found the foul-smelling scalp.

Within a few months of the War Bonnet Creek incident, that forlorn scalp ended up on display in theater lobbies as Cody's cry of triumph became a well-used line in a successful stage production, titled *The Red*

Right Hand; or *Buffalo Bill's First Scalp for Custer*. Wearing the same clothing he had donned when he killed the Cheyenne — a Mexican vaquero outfit of black velvet with scarlet sash, silver buttons, and lace trim — Buffalo Bill nightly repeated the grisly act, in what was described as a "realistic Western drama." With the passage of time, the truth became blurred. Cody's legendary confrontation evolved into a lengthy hand-to-hand battle with tomahawk and knife while almost thirty thousand hostile Indians looked on. By 1913, Buffalo Bill had reenacted the scalping in his film *The Indian Wars*.

Long after Buffalo Bill's death in 1917, the controversy over Cody's "first scalp for Custer" still festers like an open sore on a cow pony. It seems that squabbles over the details will never quit. Some of his critics question whether Cody was even involved directly in the scalping of a Cheyenne warrior. They suggest that Cody probably purchased a scalp souvenir for a few dollars from some soldier, took credit for the act of revenge, and then used the bizarre prop for his melodramas. Other credible historians point out that besides losing his hair that morning, the Cheyenne also lost his true identity. The name of the warrior was *Hay-o-wei*, which translates to Yellow Hair, for a blond scalp that the Indian had taken from a frontier victim.

Whether it was Yellow Hair or Yellow Hand who was shot and killed that hot July morning in 1876, and no matter if the person who scalped him was Buffalo Bill Cody or not, an old scalp is still on display at the Buffalo Bill Museum, at Cody, Wyoming.

And in the far reaches of Nebraska, travelers can pause at two stone markers. One of them is in memory of the troopers of the Fifth Cavalry who fought in the skirmish at War Bonnet Creek. The other obelisk marks the place where it is said that Buffalo Bill Cody took the "first scalp for Custer" — just one of many deeds that validated Cody's link between the authentic American West and the mythical Wild West of dime novels and melodramas.

Cody is not only a frontiersman, but a man of culture as well — indeed, something of a courtier. . . . But, above all, the still straight, lithe hero of a hundred border dramas is a reality, a breathing proof of the buckskin chivalry which once supplied practically all that was romantic and picturesque in American history.

— *New York Press,* 1909

Zozobra

A giant puppet effigy created by artist Will Shuster in 1926, still burned at Santa Fe's annual fiesta celebration to mark the bloodless reconquest of the city in 1692 by General Don Diego de Vargas Zapata Ponce de León. Sometimes referred to as "Old Man Gloom," this symbol of the city, consumed in flames, signifies the official beginning of fiesta.

▪

On a September Sabbath, we went deep into eastern Oklahoma, to the forest home of Cherokee Chief Wilma Mankiller and her husband, Charlie Soap. Family and friends from afar had gathered there, and over a rib feast, we talked of politics, books, recent events, and imminent change. It was well after nightfall when we formed a caravan and motored down back roads snaking through dark woods and fields along the paths "Pretty Boy" Floyd had taken when he went home. We drove beneath a heaven loaded with stars and possibilities.

At last we came to an old Cherokee stomp dance ground. Before we parked in a field of tall grass, we heard the music of chanting dancers. We walked past open shelters and tents where family meals were being prepared and babies slept. Strings of yellow lightbulbs glowed, and the smell of smoke from cooking fires permeated the night air.

Native people from different tribes had gathered to dance and celebrate. They came to remember. In the midst of a plot of ground tramped smooth as stone by generations of dancing feet burned a holy fire. Men, women, and children circled the sacred flames. The poetry of ancient songs blended with the beat of the drum and the steady rhythm from shell shakers. Flashlight beams aimed by some of the dancers in the outer circle cut through the blackness outside the fire's glow. Men and boys in jeans and caps or cowboy hats spiked with feathers joined women and girls, some of them wrapped in blankets, to move as one in layers of living rings around the fire.

We sat beneath a clan arbor with Gloria Steinem and talked of our mutual friend, Wilma Mankiller, and how they had come to know each other. Later, on the recorded tape of that conversation, we could hear the haunting chants and music of the night behind our voices. It was potent and compelling. It was divine. We will always see the embers breaking free from the flames and shooting up past the great oaks into the night. That image reminds us that fire truly is the silent language of the stars.

The dancing never stopped through the many hours we remained. When we left the grounds, we drove home through the shadowy moonlight. In our hearts was all that had been revealed to us in the flames of the sacred fire. In our minds was the poetry of the stories we had heard, especially an old Cherokee man's sweet reminiscence of when he was young, and the morning he saw "Pretty Boy" walking through the wet fields close to where we stood. They had waved at each other, the old man told us. They had exchanged smiles.

Within days of that stomp dance, we found ourselves hundreds of miles away, putting to rest a homestead in El Paso. The familiar house high above the border city on Rim Road, built fifty-five years before, had been sold, ending a long episode of family history. Memories were packed in cartons along with lamps and photographs. Furniture and dreams were carted off to other parts of the country. Hands caressed walls and doors one last time. Chimes were memorized. From the front porch, eyes scanned the sun-bleached cityscape, transformed each night by lights and moonglow into a shimmering desert diamond. Lingering ghosts were set free and invited to join us elsewhere.

We journeyed to Santa Fe for more good-byes and to pay tribute to our old friend Al Licklider, who had died of a heart attack. We, along with so many others who had loved him, delivered a tribute to Al's memory from the stage of the theatre where he had worked his sorcery. We spoke of the zany and peculiar impresario — the Pisces king. He had always resided in a dominion reserved for Merlin and Barnum and Houdini. Even the name given to him seventy-nine springs past fit so well. Alfred — from the Old English, meaning *elf*, and having the connotation of wise and clever.

His body was given to medicine. There was no coffin, no urn of ashes, no sprays of gladiolus, no sad hymns. Instead, we all told our stories, and we knew Al was there watching and listening from the wings of the theatre.

The night we left Santa Fe, we went to see Zozobra. It was the first night of fiesta, and to dispel all the worries and woes of the past year, the celebrants first had to torch Zozobra and rid themselves of Old Man Gloom. A large crowd had gathered at Fort Marcy Park for the deathwatch. They were ready to see the giant papier-mâché and muslin effigy perish.

But before the workers began to pull the hidden ropes to make the monster's thick arms and great jaws rise and fall, before the white-sheeted glooms appeared to circle and bow and pay homage, before the nimble fire dancer, with torch in hand, moved forward to ignite tumbleweeds piled around Zozobra, before the frenzied crowd shouted "Burn! Burn! Burn!" and before the fireworks exploded from his huge head, we took our leave.

We walked hand in hand away from the fiesta mob. We stopped at the post office and worked the worn combination

lock of Al's postal box. The door opened, and we thrust our hands inside. This was where he had come on daily missions for more than thirty years to hunt for checks to keep his theatrical work going. This was where he had looked for bookings from agents. This was where he had reached for connections from the world outside his magic kingdom. We invited Al to join us, but we knew he would decline. He would stay in Santa Fe.

As we drove away from the plaza, we heard the cheers of the crowd at Fort Marcy Park. Zozobra was in full flame. His groans had changed to screams. Old Man Gloom was dying.

On the highway to Albuquerque, we watched the evening sky unfold. Stars came out of nowhere. But they were no surprise; we knew they were coming. We had heard them in the fire at the Cherokee stomp dance, and again that very night, when Zozobra died.

A new week was ready to begin. Promise and hope rode the night breezes. In the rearview mirror, we watched the glow of Santa Fe for many miles, until we were swallowed by the adobe hills. Above the high desert, a new moon showed the way, and we listened to the lucky stars all the way home.

ABOUT THE AUTHORS

Michael Wallis is a native of Missouri, and has lived and worked throughout the West. His work has been published in hundreds of magazines and newspapers. His best-selling books include: *Oil Man: The Story of Frank Phillips and the Birth of Phillips Petroleum*; *Route 66: The Mother Road*; *Pretty Boy: The Life and Times of Charles Arthur Floyd*; *Way Down Yonder in the Indian Nation: Writings From America's Heartland*; *Mankiller: A Chief and Her People*; *En Divina Luz: The Penitente Moradas of New Mexico*; and *Beyond the Hills: The Journey of Waite Phillips*.

Michael was a nominee for the National Book Award and has been thrice nominated for the Pulitzer Prize. He has received many other prestigious honors, including the Lynn Riggs Award, and was the first inductee into the Oklahoma Route 66 Hall of Fame.

Suzanne Fitzgerald Wallis, a native Texan, also has lived and worked in the West and abroad. Her writing and photography have been published in countless books, magazines, and newspapers. Suzanne has helped produce and narrate several video projects and documentary films about Route 66 and other subjects.

As president and founder of the Wallis Group, Suzanne heads up a public relations and editorial marketing firm in Tulsa, Oklahoma. In addition to national corporate accounts, her agency has represented several major publishing houses and spearheaded a special project for the American Booksellers Association.

Michael and Suzanne, best friends since 1968, were married in 1982. They serve as editors for Songdog Books, a Council Oak imprint. They have worked together on several literary projects since 1970, when they founded *Esperanza: A Quarterly of Literature and Art* in Santa Fe, New Mexico. In 1993, St. Martin's Press published *Route 66 Postcards: Greetings from the Mother Road*, a series of thirty vintage postcards from the Wallis collection.

Michael and Suzanne are frequent public speakers and have led several tours down Route 66 for the Smithsonian Institution, the National Trust for Historic Preservation, and the University Center at Tulsa. They maintain a home in Tulsa, and a songdog hideout in northern New Mexico.